Adolescent Medicine

Based on a conference organised by the
Royal College of Physicians of London

Edited by

Aidan Macfarlane

*Director of the National Adolescent and
Student Health Unit, Oxford*

1996

**ROYAL COLLEGE OF PHYSICIANS
OF LONDON**

Acknowledgement

The Royal College of Physicians acknowledges with thanks a grant from the Virgin Healthcare Foundation towards the cost of producing this book.

Royal College of Physicians of London
11 St Andrews Place, London NW1 4LE

Registered Charity No. 210508

Copyright © 1996 Royal College of Physicians of London
ISBN 1 86016 025 5

Typeset by Dan-Set Graphics, Telford, Shropshire
Printed in Great Britain by The Lavenham Press Ltd, Lavenham, Sudbury, Suffolk

Foreword

Adolescence is the space of life between the ages of 10 and 19, between childhood and maturity. It is a time when the body reaches physical perfection but it is also a time when, as Keats wrote as a 23 year-old in *Endymion*: 'The soul is in ferment, the character undecided, the way of life uncertain, the ambition thickset'. Those of us who are accustomed to dealing with the medical problems of childhood or later age are lulled by these young people's apparent health into paying less attention than they deserve to their very real health needs; and we are taken aback when we discover how much such social and psychological factors affect the health of young men and women as they pass from childhood to maturity.

Adolescent health matters—to the young people themselves, their parents and families, their teachers and future employers, and to society as a whole. This book reflects the concerns of a diverse group of health professionals—doctors, nurses, social workers and administrators—who came together under the aegis of the Royal College of Physicians to examine the medical problems created by the use of illegal drugs, suicides, accidents, sexual exploration, AIDS, smoking, alcohol, depression or by common diseases, and to discuss ways to achieve a healthier life for these young people. They are the next generation of decision-makers and anyone who cares for the future health of the nation—from community nurses, through primary health care doctors, to those in the tertiary services—must take a serious interest in adolescent health matters. I believe this book will be a valuable contribution to the subject.

LESLIE TURNBERG
President of the Royal College of Physicians

March 1996

iii

Contributors

Priscilla Alderson BA PhD *Senior Research Officer, Social Science Research Unit, Institute of Education, 18 Woburn Square, London WC1H 0NS*

Christine Baker MN RGN RM RSCN *Senior Nurse, Rainbow Children and Young Persons Unit, Royal Gwent Hospital, Glan Hafran NHS Trust, Cardiff Road, Newport NP9 2UB*

Elizabeth C Crowne MD MRCP *Clinical Lecturer in Paediatric Endocrinology, Level 4, University of Oxford Department of Paediatrics, John Radcliffe Hospital, Headington, Oxford OX3 9DU*

David B Dunger MD FRCP *Consultant Paediatric Endocrinologist, Level 4, University of Oxford Department of Paediatrics, John Radcliffe Hospital, Headington, Oxford OX3 9DU*

Stephen A Greene MB BS FRCP(Ed) *Consultant in Paediatric Endocrinology, Department of Paediatrics, Ninewells Hospital and Medical School, Dundee DD1 9SY*

Keith Hawton DM FRCPsych *Consultant Psychiatrist and Senior Clinical Lecturer, University Department of Psychiatry, Warneford Hospital , Oxford OX3 7JX*

Zarrina Kurtz MB FRCP FFPHM *Consultant in Public Health and Health Policy, 12 Blithfield Street, London W8 6RH; previously: Directorate of Health Policy and Public Health, South West Thames Regional Health Authority, 40 Eastbourne Terrace, London W2 3QR*

Aidan Macfarlane MB FRCP *Director, National Adolescent and Student Health Unit, PO Box 777, Oxford OX3 7LF*

Ann McPherson MB BS DCH FRCGP *General Practitioner, 19 Beaumont Street, Oxford OX1 2NA*

Leon Polnay MB BS DCH FRCP *Honorary Consultant Community Paediatrician and Reader in Child Health, Department of Child Health, Floor E East Block, University Hospital, Queen's Medical Centre, Nottingham NG7 2UH*

Philip Robson MB BS MRCP(UK) MRCPsych *Consultant Psychiatrist and Senior Clinical Lecturer, Chilton Clinic, Warneford Hospital, Warneford Lane, Headington, Oxford OX3 7JX*

Terence J Ryan DM FRCP *Clinical Professor of Dermatology, Dermatology Department, The Churchill Hospital, Old Road, Headington, Oxford OX3 7LJ*

Jo Sibert MD FRCP *Professor of Community Child Health, University of Wales College of Medicine, University Department of Child Health, Llandough Special Children's Centre, Penlan Road, Penarth, S Glam CF64 2XX*

Hilarie Williams MB BS DCH MRCP(UK) MRCGP *Senior Medical Officer, Department of Health, Wellington House, 133-155 Waterloo Road, London SE1 8UG*

Contents

PART 4: Psychological aspects of adolescence

Introduction

Illegal drugs, sex, pregnancies, depression, suicide, alcohol and cigarettes, accidents—all this may sound like the average contents of a blockbuster novel, but it is also a shortlist of the challenges and hazards facing the adolescent in Britain today. Professional, parent or guardian—if you have a role caring for adolescents then these are the issues with which you need to be familiar.

As stated in the Foreword to this book, adolescent health matters. We know what the problems are and how they affect the transition of the teenager into adulthood. Now we also need answers as to where health professionals fit in, how do they dovetail with the family and ensure that the care that they are providing is effective. The key is communication—keeping the channels open is our best way of making sure adolescent problems are not ignored, and to leave behind the mindset that says talking to 'difficult' teenagers is impossible—it isn't.

As medicine becomes more sophisticated we must adapt to the needs of specific client groups. Adolescent health is a newly emerged area of interest which everyone working in child and adult health fields should know about—from community nurses, through the primary health care team on to the tertiary services. This book is directly concerned with helping you meet the health and social care needs of adolescents, by defining the medical problems and suggesting solutions which will hopefully make that forementioned list of potential challenges to the health and well-being of young people much less damaging.

April 1996

AIDAN MACFARLANE
Editor

PART ONE

Defining the
medical problems

1 | Health and illness in adolescents: a national overview

Hilarie Williams

Senior Medical Officer, Department of Health, London

This chapter sets out some of the most important areas of health, or lack of health, in the adolescent population. In doing so it will draw heavily on information presented in the Chief Medical Officer's report *On the State of the Public Health* for 1993.[1] The report included a chapter on the health of adolescents which has acted as a catalyst to the development of public health interest in this area. This chapter is devoted to a few major topics which generally coincide with those key areas of the Health of the Nation strategy[2] with immediate relevance to the health of young people.

The word 'adolescents' will be used to refer to young people aged between 10 and 19 years since this has been the definition employed by the World Health Organisation since 1988.[3] Using this definition, the estimated population of adolescents in England was nearly 7½ million in 1982.[4] This had, however, dropped to about 5.8 million by 1992.[5] This contrasted with an overall increase in population size so that the proportion of the general population made up by adolescents fell from 16% to 12% in that time.[4,5] This reduction in the proportion of adolescents as a total of the population reflects a downward trend in family size which was probably accentuated by a shift in the late 1970s and early 1980s towards later childbearing. That shift in childbearing age has only had a temporary effect so the numbers are set to recover somewhat in the early part of the 21st century and the Government Actuary's Department's projection for 2002 is some 6.4 million adolescents in England with a projection for 2012 of approximately 6.5 million.[6]

Adolescent mortality data

The topics of most immediate concern when dealing with adolescent health and illness are those which arise from the mortality data. The death of a young person becomes arguably more poignant where that death could have been prevented. Mortality data are the most robust data which we have on a national scale and show that by far and away the major category of cause of death in adolescents is 'injury and poisoning'; that is a category which one might argue to be largely 'avoidable'. In 1992, there were 1,021 deaths in adolescents in England and Wales attributed to injury and poisoning and, of these, three-quarters were in males.[7] What is good is that this number contrasted with 1,820 such deaths in 1982.[8] This reduction does, however, reinforce the avoidable nature of many of these deaths so it should act as a spur to further prevention activities.

Accidents

'Injury and poisoning' is a category which includes suicide and homicide but it is dominated by accidents, the first of the key areas of the Health of the Nation dealt with here. The first two targets for accidents are: to reduce the death rate for accidents among children aged under 15 by at least 33% by 2005 (baseline 1990) and to reduce the death rate for accidents among young people aged 15–24 by at least 25% by 2005 (baseline 1990). Both of these cover people in the adolescent age range and, in line with the overall diminution in deaths from injury and poisoning, we have already achieved some 9% of the 33% target for reduction in deaths among those under 15 and 4.8% towards the 25% target for reductions in deaths among 15 to 24 year olds by 1992.[8,9] Although statistics for 1993 are available, the classifications have changed so, until more data have been collected, it will not be possible to comment accurately on the trend after 1992.[10]

Obviously, not all accidents are fatal but at present there are no overall national data for morbidity from accidents. The Health of the Nation key area handbook on accidents[11] lists sources of data on accidents, namely the Home Office (Fire Brigade fire statistics; the Police 'Stats 19' returns relating to road accidents); Department of Trade and Industry Home Accident Surveillance System and Leisure Accidents Surveillance System; the Office of Population Censuses and Surveys (OPCS) which conducts *ad hoc* surveys as well as providing mortality data; the National Poisons Information Service and the Royal Society for the Prevention of Accidents which collects data on drowning. A national taskforce is looking at ways of using information from these various sources to provide national data on non-fatal accidents.

Mention of accidents has to consider the contribution of alcohol—estimated to be a factor in 30% of accidents. This refers to

all age groups but it has also been estimated that alcohol con-
tributes to 60% of fatal accidents in young men occurring
between 10 p.m. and 4 a.m.[11] Various surveys have revealed that a
large number of young teenagers are regular drinkers.[5,6] For
example, the Health Education Authority's survey *Tomorrow's
Young Adults*[12] conducted in 1992 among 9–15 year olds found that
12% drank alcohol at least weekly. Among 11–15 year olds 31%
had had a drink in the preceding week and, of these, 4% of girls
exceeded 14 units per week, the recommended level for adult
women, and 3% of boys exceeded 21 units per week—the
recommended level for adult men.

Mental illness

If one looks at the percentage changes in numbers of deaths in
adolescents between 1982 and 1992, the news tends to be good in
that, for most causes, the change has been downwards rather than
upwards. The major exception is 'mental disorders'. The actual
number of deaths from mental disorders is small, for example 53
in 1992.[7] But even allowing for the effects of small numbers, there
has been a marked increase since 1982[8] when there were only 20
such deaths. The 53 deaths in 1992 comprised 45 attributed to
drug dependence, 7 attributed to non-dependent drug abuse and
1 attributed to 'mental retardation'. The corresponding figures for
1982 were 14, 4 and 2.

Mental health and illness among young people is a major issue
for the Department of Health. With the Department for Education, the Department of Health has recently issued a handbook on
child and adolescent mental health services[13] which draws heavily
on a national review of services by Kurtz, Thornes and Wolkind[14]
and an epidemiologically based needs assessment by Wallace *et
al.*[15] It suggests that some 10–20% of children will, at some time,
have a problem severe enough to require specialist help and that
some 10–20% of adolescents will have some mental health problems in any one year, although the majority of those will not need
specialist professional help. The preliminary data from Wallace *et
al.* include prevalence estimates of: 2–8% for major depression;
1.9% for excessive compulsive disorders; 1.3% for encopresis for
boys aged 11–12; 0.5–1% for anorexia nervosa in the 12–19 age
group and 1% for bulimia nervosa in girls. It is estimated that
2–4% of adolescents have attempted suicide at some time and that
7.6 people per 100,000 in the age range 15–19 do commit suicide
each year.

Suicide

Deaths from suicide are categorised with deaths from 'injury and poisoning' but the overall reduction in deaths from injury and poisoning masks a less optimistic picture for deaths from suicide, particularly for young men.

Suicide and attempted suicide are the subject of another chapter in this book but it is worth noting that those at increased risk include previous suicide attempters and those with a history of alcohol or drug misuse. Suicides among young men have shown an upward trend since the early 1970s and this compares with a fairly stable picture in young women.

Deaths from cancer

The second largest category for deaths in 10–19 year olds is death from cancers. There were 263 deaths from cancer in adolescents in England and Wales in 1992[7] but this is only a partial indicator of the morbidity associated with neoplasia as there are roughly 900 new cancer registrations per year in England and Wales in this age group. These registrations are dominated by leukaemias and lymphomas followed by brain tumours. Cancer is a key area of the strategy for health but, obviously, the health promotion activities directed at adolescents in this context are aiming to prevent cancer in later life.

HIV/AIDS and sexual health

There are some parallels here with another key area 'HIV/AIDS and sexual health' in that, with the exception of those infected through blood and blood products, very few cases of AIDS have been diagnosed in adolescents, but it is extremely important to provide health promotion to this age group because of the potential for long-term effects of high risk behaviour. Up to the end of 1994[16] there had been only some 58 cases of AIDS diagnosed in 15–19 year olds since 1981. However, there had been 2,251 cases of AIDS diagnosed in 20–29 year olds and, given a mean incubation period of over 10 years following transmission of infection, this implies that a relatively large number of adolescents in the UK may have been infected with HIV. Looking more generally at issues relating to sexual health there is obviously considerably more immediate impact on the adolescent, both for acute sexually transmitted diseases and unwanted pregnancies. This key area of the Health of the Nation includes a target specific to adolescents, ie to reduce by at least 50% the rate of conception amongst the under 16s by the year 2000 (baseline 1989).

The number of conceptions in under 16s rose steadily during the 1980s and although they now appear to be reducing again[17,18] the most frequent causes of hospital admission of 15–16 year old girls are termination of pregnancy or childbirth.[19]

Conclusion

To summarise, the data on mortality and the, understandably, much less complete data on morbidity reveal adolescents to have very substantial health needs. This provides us with a challenge for provision of services suited to the needs of young people. It also provides a challenge for education so that those who are healthy may stay healthy. That challenge is not only to provide appropriate information but to look at ways of making young people absorb it and act upon it.

References

1. Department of Health. *On the State of the Public Health: The Annual Report of the Chief Medical Officer of the Department of Health for the Year 1993.* London: HMSO, 1994.
2. Department of Health. *The Health of the Nation: A Strategy for Health in England.* London: HMSO, 1992.
3. World Health Organisation. *PB/90–91.* Geneva: WHO, 1988.
4. OPCS. *Population Estimates 1982.* PP1 94/1 (revised estimates).
5. OPCS. *Population Estimates 1992.* PP1 93/3.
6. Government Actuary's Department National Population Projections series PP2.
7. OPCS. *Mortality Statistics 1992.* DH2, No. 19. London: HMSO.
8. OPCS. *Mortality Statistics 1982.* DH2, No. 9. London: HMSO.
9. Department of Health. *The Health of the Nation: One Year On—A Report on the Progress of the Health of the Nation.* London: Department of Health, 1993.
10. Department of Health. *Health of the Nation: Fit for the Future—Second Progress Report on the Health of the Nation.* London: Department of Health, 1995.
11. Department of Health. *Health of the Nation Key Area Handbook: Accidents.* London: Department of Health, 1993.
12. Health Education Authority. *Tomorrow's Young Adults: 9–15 Year Olds Look at Alcohol, Drugs, Exercise and Smoking.* London: Health Education Authority, 1992.
13. Department of Health, Department for Education. *Health of the Nation: A Handbook on Child and Adolescent Mental Health.* London: Department of Health, 1995.
14. Kurtz Z, Thornes R, Wolkind S. *Services for the Mental Health of Children and Young People in England: A National Review.* South Thames Regional Health Authority, 1994.

15. Wallace SA, Crown JM, Cox AD, Berger M. *Epidemiologically Based Needs Assessment: Child and Adolescent Mental Health.* Wessex Institute of Public Health (in press).
16. Public Health Laboratories Service AIDS Centre and Scottish Centre for Infection and Environmental Health: AIDS/HIV Quarterly Surveillance Tables, No. 27.
17. OPCS. *Birth Statistics* FM1 94/1.
18. OPCS. *Population Trends* 73.
19. Henderson J, Goldacre M, Yeats D. Use of hospital inpatient care in adolescence. *Archives of Disease in Childhood* 1993; **69**: 559–63.

2 | Sociological aspects of adolescent health and illness

Priscilla Alderson
Senior Research Officer, Institute of Education, University of London

The story of adolescence began to be told about one hundred years ago. Why is it such a new story, and what happened before then? What is the story of adolescence about? Is it true? And how beneficial is it, in terms of young people's health? Like historians, sociologists study the beliefs and behaviours that shape social events. This chapter reviews some of the key beliefs in the short history of adolescence, and then questions how much we are influenced by these beliefs today.

Creating the story of adolescence

Before this century, children were treated in similar ways to adults as soon as they were old enough to work or to leave the schoolroom.[1] The aim was to enable children to achieve adult attitudes and behaviour as soon as possible. The great educator and doctor John Locke advised: 'The sooner you treat him as a man, the sooner he will be one'.[2] For centuries, young people were expected to engage in all kinds of trades and crafts, as workers in their own right. Shakespeare created all his heroines to be acted by young boys; the star parts of church music were also written for young boys. Presumably they performed with the excellence and dedication we see in young musicians, actors and sports people today. By the nineteenth century, childhood lasted longer in upper class families, but a separate stage between childhood and adulthood was scarcely considered.

In 1839, the headmaster of Rugby declared in a sermon to the school: 'the change from childhood to manhood ... ought to be hastened; and it is a sin in everyone not to hasten it'.[3] However, by then, different views were emerging. Another headmaster stated: 'How I dread mannikizing a boy. What do you say to a baby with whiskers? No, keep boys boys.' One of the main purposes of the public schools was to prolong childhood dependence and submission, though this

9

had its problems. There were revolts in the schools, and the army was summoned to quell some of these.[4]

Clearly some of the 'babies' were mature young men. The concept of *precocity* was invented so that, if young people seemed mature, this could be explained away. They could be regarded as abnormal, unhealthy, and suffering from premature growth. Experts at the time were fond of gardening metaphors, which prepared the way for the invention of the adolescent.

Other movements which have helped to create and extend the story of adolescence are:

- the state school systems from the 1880s, taking many street-wise children away from employment and adult society (and incidentally increasing their poverty);[5]
- the demands of modern industrial society for workers who have had years of schooling;
- the gradual rise in the school leaving age;
- increase in national concern about managing the health of young people and their future reproductive health;
- rising unemployment rates among adults, who prefer young people to be at college or in 'training schemes' and not competing for real jobs;
- the growth of commercially driven youth cultures;
- recent reductions in benefits for people under 25, and housing shortages which delay their move away from the parental home.

These are all broadly political and economic factors. They tell us more about the way adults manage society, than about the actual nature and abilities of young people.

However, academic and professional concern about adolescence tends to concentrate on young people's biology and emotions. In 1904 the psychologist Stanley Hall published his enormous book, *Adolescence.*[6] He wrote at length on the pilgrimage of the child soul to the man soul. He was deeply concerned, at a time in the USA of rising immigration levels, that one decade of childhood was not long enough to become a true American; two decades of preparation were necessary. Whole chapters are devoted to puberty and menstruation. When the young woman begins to menstruate, says Hall:

> She exults in her womanhood as something superior, and feels it worthy of love, reverence, protection, care, and service. In early adolescence her impulse is to make herself absolutely perfect. When her cycle is complete, her whole life must be regulated to prepare for the

next. She develops new sentiments, instincts, and insights, is a charm
to herself and both a fascination and a study for others ... Every day of
the 28 she is a different being ...

The stages of shock, hysteria, joy and pain are meticulously recorded. If study or exercise interfere with the cycle, they must be sus-
pended. Regularity over 28 days was thought to be essential. Doctors hung over the beds of young women urging them to
menstruate.[7] In cases of irregularity, they resorted to D&Cs in
efforts to stave off the serious sequelae of amenorrhoea, which
included abnormal brain conditions.[6]

Hall was influenced by the psychiatrist Henry Maudsley, who
believed that crime 'indicated a congenital fault of mental organisation ... a failure of the brain to function properly'.[8] Maudsley
identified menstruation, pregnancy and lactation as causes of
insanity and crime 'attributable to irritation of the ovaries or
uterus, a disease by which the chaste and modest woman is transformed into a raging fury of lust'. Hall also refers to Havelock Ellis,
who described 'the criminal type' which, he considered, 'resem-
bled the Mongoloid or sometimes the Negroid', morally and physically 'peculiar'. He examined numerous prisoners and noted their
abnormal genitalia, menstrual changes and 'orgies' which included attempts to break out of prison. Historians of Ellis ask what evidence was available for comparison with 'normal' non-criminal
women, and how much of this science was voyeurism or
pornography.

Hall's vast atlas of adolescence mapped out the domain to which
many 'experts' expected all young people to conform. It inspired
Cyril Burt's book *The Young Delinquent*[9] about young people who
were referred to him for offences such as theft or 'excessive bad
temper', or 'willing sexual relations'. Burt and Ellis began to
'define and map sexual behaviour' and they claimed to define
'normal' and 'abnormal' activity and appearance.[8] They recorded
many examples of young working class women, noting their ugli-
ness, their 'fierce' features and the marks of a 'hopeless moral
reprobate'. They forged further links between delinquency, menstruation and 'sexual excitement' in their records of girls who
would run away, wander the streets late at night, accost strange
men and have frequent outbreaks of temper. There is no hint in
their records of the starvation wages paid, for example, to seam-
stresses or of the pressures on them to resort to prostitution and
self-defence as means of survival. Burt believed that these 'very
dangerous' girls should be confined in colonies to a state of childhood under the supervision of 'house parents'. In 1932 a report by

Burt's colleague for the Medical Research Council recommended supervision from psychologists for these girls, permanent segregation and sterilisation. Working class areas should be allocated as 'hunting grounds' for research psychologists to select cases who 'from that time onward would come under the sole guardianship of the investigator'.[10]

There is not space here to review the following 60 years, or to trace the links between earlier and current views of adolescence. There have been many changes but there are also common themes. Though now less explicitly stated, there is still much concern about adolescence as a time of extra problems:

- physical problems of growth, accidents and injuries, anorexia or obesity;
- sexual problems of abortion, pregnancy, sexually transmitted diseases;
- emotional problems of depression, self-obsession, anxiety, and being moody, labile, demanding, rebellious and unpredictable;
- social problems of rising rates of crime and homelessness, school refusal and exclusion, alcohol and drug misuse, exploitation from the consumerist youth culture, being hostage to peer approval, and so on.

There is also concern about the 'tasks' adolescents perform: surviving puberty, starting work or youth training or college, forming sexual partnerships.

Adolescents are believed to have lost some of the innocence of childhood, but to need protection from the full rigours of adulthood. The academic literature, texts for practitioners, the mass media and public opinion all provide countless examples of the story of adolescence. The accounts stress that young people are inexperienced, ignorant, dependent, unreliable, irresponsible, easily misled and often foolish. In sum, they are incompetent and need adult guidance and control. At a recent conference on adolescents, a psychologist suggested that every adolescent who requires any kind of hospital treatment should also see a psychologist, for help with the problems of being adolescent—as if it is a kind of sickness.

The racist beliefs of Hall, Ellis and Burt have been quoted partly because these pervade their work, partly because similar beliefs inspired the imperialist efforts of explorers, missionaries and merchants in the colonies for over 500 years. In this tradition, Hall's book on adolescence opened up a new land for the modern explorers (or researchers), the missionaries (people working in adolescent health and education) and, more recently, in consumer societies, the merchants (such as of fashion and music).

This sense of civilised adults entering alien territory accentuates current themes in the story of adolescence:

- it is a time of extra risk to health and safety because of immaturity;
- adolescents need missionary style health care and education to alter their creeds and codes and to rescue them from harms they are too weak and ignorant to resist;
- they need time to evolve or develop into adulthood;
- anything they do (school work, work experience, weekend jobs) does not count as real work but as learning or practising;[11]
- their sexual relationships are 'risk-taking' or 'experiment' and cannot be deep, lasting or sincere;
- it is foolish or cruel to expect too much from them;
- without guidance from expert professionals, they are unable to steer through the troubled waters of adolescence into the relative calm of adult life.

Is the story true?

The accuracy of the story of adolescence can be checked by asking: How valid are the theories and beliefs on which it is based? How nearly do the accounts tally with everyday evidence? How do they fit with up-to-date, systematic records and research evidence?

Recapitulation

Hall claimed that his theories were scientific and unbiased. Yet his prejudices concerning race, class, misogyny and eugenics are strikingly apparent today. Although he refers to Darwin, he ignores Darwin's thesis that evolution occurs extremely slowly over many generations. Hall invoked earlier unscientific beliefs about *recapitulation*, the idea that each person relives the history of the race from savage childhood (allusions here to pygmies, hunter-gatherers and primitive races), through the neo-atavistic storm-and-stress period of adolescence, to the higher stage of civilised adulthood. This hypothesis influences psychology and public opinion so powerfully (then and now) that Hall was able to cite numerous researchers and theorists to support his views. Yet their work is founded on fallacy; recapitulation, among other theories, has been criticised as the 'rotten' foundations of child development.[12]

Child development

Adolescence is part 2 of the three part human story, which assumes that there are clear differences between child (very undeveloped), adolescent (partly developed) and adult (the endpoint, informed, wise, mature, dependable). However, part 1, child development, does not withstand critical scrutiny. For example, the myth that babies start at a very low point and slowly advance in every respect is challenged by everyday evidence and systematic research. Babies engage in sophisticated forms of communication;[13] young children can deal with complex cognitive and moral ideas.[14] Research in homes and schools shows how much young children have in common with adults, and how sensitively they can respond to other people's feelings.[15] Norwegian children aged from 3 years have 'sweethearts', play kissing games and negotiate that 'floating level between friendship and affection',[16] supposedly the province of adolescence. Four year old girls, tape-recorded talking at home and at school, used complex language, concepts, logic and arguments.[17] Research in homes, schools and day care centres shows that children are far more advanced than laboratory-based research and rigid tests and experiments suggest. News reports and media events show children behaving in ways we think of as 'adult', such as the 'children of courage' awards, the estimated 10,000 children who are the main carer for a sick or disabled relative in the UK, and the young teenagers who head households in countries with AIDS epidemics.

The ideal adult

Part 3 of the human story is equally dubious. Are adults always wise, informed, stable and responsible? Do adults or adolescents cause the greatest disruption in terms of traffic accidents, 'manmade' famine and ecological disaster, war, economic inequality leading to disease and disability, and so on? Why do we label adult expressions of emotion or selfishness as 'the child within us' or 'being adolescent' instead of recognising that at every age we have mixed capacities: rational and impulsive, wise and foolish, selfish and altruistic?

Binary ways of thinking (such as that someone is either an adolescent or an adult, either wise or foolish) have great advantages as the foundations of modern science, technology and philosophy. Yet they also have disadvantages. They oversimplify complex realities. Groups of people tend to be defined by what is supposed to divide them in their class, ethnicity, sex, ability and age. Similarities are discounted. Superior qualities then tend to be ascribed to one group, such as wisdom, maturity and competence to adults, whereas inferior qualities are assigned to the opposite group, children and teenagers. Public prejudice fuels and is reinforced by academic and professional theory.

Splitting and projection

Splitting and projection occur when adults unrealistically fail to acknowledge their own weaknesses and then project them onto children, and when adults overestimate their own strengths and deny those of young people. One example is when Hall, Maudsley, Ellis and Burt pathologised lower class young women's sexuality and appeared blind to their own peculiarities. The splitting is often less blatant, but can still mean that both sides tend to miss out. The 'mature' people are less able to laugh, have fun and be impulsive ('men don't cry'); if people who are seen as 'immature' try to be responsible they are called unnatural or disobedient. The exaggerated split between adult and child is still very widely accepted, and prevents us from seeing children as real people in their own right, and yet the fallacies in parts 1 and 3 of the human story undermine the credibility of part 2, adolescence.

Fact and fiction

A further illusion in the story of adolescence appears when it is told as if it is a true story. This occurs when adolescence is described in terms of a biological state of prolonged puberty or an inevitable psychological process, if it is presented as a universal phenomenon occurring in every culture and century, or as defined by infallible expert knowledge, or when difficulties experienced by a tiny minority of young people are generally attributed to the whole group. These approaches to adolescence ignore two inevitable complications in such accounts: *perception* and *reaction*.

Perceptions. As already discussed, adolescence tends to be perceived through layers of tradition and prejudice, and it is often hard for people to distinguish their own expectations from the evidence. With my colleague Jill Siddle, I interviewed over 300 children and adults in hospitals, asking them about when they thought that young people could be informed and rational enough to make decisions about proposed major surgery.[18] The replies ranged from early childhood to 'never'. They often told us more about the interviewee's perceptions, than about children's actual abilities.

Reactions. Another complication in standard accounts of adolescence is that they implicitly portray young people as puppets, twitched by the strings of biology and culture. This rather passive model ignores the ways in which human beings act and react. Research with 10 to 12 year olds in Norway documents how children who are respected and encouraged to be competent take on major responsibilities, and grow in maturity and confidence. Those who are treated as incompetent remain so.[19] Attempts to measure adolescents' abilities have to take account of the social context, including relationships between the assessors and the young people. Children's sensitive reactions to Piaget's repetitive questions (when he kept asking the same question they may have politely assumed that he wanted different answers) have been suggested as a reason why he found them to be much less competent than later researchers have found.[20] Human relations, including those between young people and adults who test them, are dynamic not static; people interact through mutually reinforcing expectations. Although this is still so seldom acknowledged, it was recognised sixty years ago in this unusually positive account:

> Boys and girls learn from one another, testing precepts, breaking away from parental teachings, modifying and remoulding attitudes in the light of others of their own age. But for this leavening trend, the new generation would be but a replica of the old, and social progress would once more be slowed down. The brevity of the phase of adolescence has its tragic aspects for society is badly in need of the qualities which belong to youth, high ideals, faith in our own ability, courage to follow our best beliefs. Too much vitality is drained off in the struggle between old and young, we need understanding and tolerance.[21]

This aspect of youth could be far more widely appreciated, whereas, at present, to describe someone as 'adult' tends to be a compliment, to call them 'adolescent' tends to be an insult. Its murky origins still cling to the concept of adolescence, which is used to make misleading generalisations about young people that ignore the powerful influences of prejudged perceptions and the possibility of changing reactions in human affairs.

How does the story of adolescence promote young people's health?

The concept of adolescence is supposed to enable young people to enjoy extra protection and services. On balance, does this do more good or harm? The teen years are unusually healthy ones,[22] so it is odd that extra health services should be expected for them. Most of the disease is social rather than biological in origin, and linked to depression, anxiety, accidents and violence. For example, many people are depressed about overcrowded housing and violence in the family. A common medical response is to try to palliate the emotional ill effects, to treat each case in isolation from the social context, to offer help such as counselling instead of rehousing. The idea that doctors have nothing to do with housing policy is questionable, when they spend so much time grappling with the emotional effects of poor housing.

This kind of palliation is arguably unscientific and unsatisfactory medicine on four grounds: it addresses the symptoms instead of the disease; it offers only temporary palliation in lieu of more lasting cure or prevention; it perceives each case in isolation instead of recognising trends and even epidemics of commonly shared stressors; it is prone to victim blaming, seeing the origins as well as the effects of this dis-ease within the patient. A major question for everyone who works with and cares for young people is: how much does the story of adolescence create and compound the very problems which adults are trying to alleviate?

Imagine that you have a cousin aged 40, whose successful business suddenly collapses. He becomes bankrupt, his house is repossessed and his family leave him. He asks to live with you for a while. Gradually the arguments start when you come home tired from work:

> Can't you even wash up your coffee cups? You've got nothing else to do. Why don't you get a job? Why do you go down to the pub and waste your benefit? You should stay in and get on with that expensive correspondence course I've paid for. I don't care if you think it's boring, that's your only hope for the future. In another two or three years when you've got a proper income, that's the time when you can begin to think about enjoying yourself, not now. How dare you borrow my car, after all I've done for you! If you're depressed you've only yourself to blame. Stop being such a hopeless slob...

The rows become more furious and violent until the GP or the police are called in or the cousin leaves. How many adults would stay calm under these restrictions which are accepted as routine for teenagers? Adolescence literally means 'becoming adult'. It can be used to mean 'put your life on hold until you can enjoy adult freedoms, income and authority'. This presupposes that young people, though fully developed physically and intellectually, are more like dependent young children than healthy adults. Given the restrictions placed on capable young people, it is not surprising that fully healthy fulfilment is widely identified with adulthood. For example, the Court Report on child health services was written by people who were especially concerned with children's best interests. Yet they chose the title *Fit for the Future* which implies a latent childhood and a fulfilled adulthood. The opening words identify real health with adulthood, 'By health, I mean the power to live a full, adult, living, breathing life, in close contact with what I love—I want to be all that I am capable of becoming'.[23]

Teenage pregnancy

Among many examples, teenage pregnancy illustrates how concepts of adolescence can oppress and harm young people.[24] Most teenage mothers are aged 18 and 19. They have already left school and tend to have been unemployed or in unrewarding work. Instead of seeing pregnancy as interrupting their education or careers, they tend to say that they prefer child care to the dull work they did before. Having children often leads them later into more rewarding employment. Many women are still as poor in their twenties and thirties as in their teens; for them, arguments against having a child until they can 'afford' one could mean never being able to have children. There are advantages when young mothers still have very close contact with the extended family who share in supporting and caring for the mother and baby. Research suggests that young mothers receive far more help from their relatives than from health visitors or social workers. They are accused of 'being dependent', though all adults who stay at home to look after small children are dependent on some other wage earner or the state. The real accusation seems to be that younger mothers are more likely to depend on benefits, instead of on private income from a partner, and this can apply to mothers in every age group. The term 'teenage mothers' can be a crude label for a very diverse group of young women. Mothers aged 18 can have far more in common with those aged 28, than with those aged 14. There is no clear evidence that younger mothers are better or worse parents than older ones or, when socioeconomic groups are compared, that deferring childbearing beyond the teenage years is necessarily any better for women and children. With regard to physical health, many health problems associated with poverty increase with age. It is possible that the younger disadvantaged women are when they have babies, the better the outcome is likely to be for mother and baby.[25] 'Teenage mothers' were fully accepted in UK and US society until as recently as the 1960s, when liberals began to think that teenagers should not have babies and conservatives thought that they should not have sex.[26]

Life can be very tough because young mothers are trapped in the double standards of a permissive yet prudish society. Casual sex is accepted in the media and used to sell anything, but there are restrictions on the advertising of contraceptives. Young mothers face enormous problems of poverty and discrimination. However, their difficulties are not really due to their age or confined to their age group. Although early pregnancy is associated with poverty, there is no evidence that it causes poverty. Marriage would not make many of these young mothers any richer, and there is little reason to believe their situation will improve as they get older, even if they deferred pregnancy. The best way to help young mothers is to stop seeing them as a social problem, and to see them instead as mothers with problems 'often not of their own making—who are struggling gainst the odds. Most fare well under difficult circumstances' (Phoenix,[24] p.253).

Physical punishment

It is illegal to touch adults without their consent; physical punishment in the armed services and in prisons has gradually been abandoned. The only people who can still legally be hit are children, by people with parental authority, childminders who have the parents' permission and private school teachers. The double standard that forbids hitting of adults but allows it for children is justified by traditional beliefs about rational adults who must be in control and irrational children who understand a smack but not reasoning. As briefly reviewed above, these beliefs are refuted by evidence of young children's reasoning abilities. The Health Visitors Association considers that society's tolerance of the double standard increases the incidence of child abuse and injury and homelessness when teenagers run away from violent homes. The Association considers the problem to be so serious that it must be addressed in general, political terms, and supports End Physical Punishment of Children (EPPOCH), the movement to change the law and to end physical punishment of children. However, the British Paediatric Association continues to support the story of adolescence that young people require different treatment from adults.[27] One way to challenge violence against children is to demonstrate how mature they can be when they are respected. This approach works to break down false ideas about the supposed great differences between adults and children which use of the term adolescence reinforces.

Health services for young people

When the concept of a separate adolescent group is questioned, new approaches to their health care can be considered. These include trying to treat people in every age group with respect, and to address the actual problems instead of the symptoms. From many possible examples, here are a few.

If teenagers find GP surgeries unwelcoming, instead of trying to provide alternative services, change the surgery to make it more welcoming to everyone. If people aged 16 are intimidated, people aged 80 are also likely to be. If shops and sports centres can offer user-friendly services to all age groups surely the health services can too.

People with long-term illnesses and disability can be very distressed about having to spend so much time attending clinics. Joint clinics held nearer their home are helpful, and so are staff who recognise that teenagers take, or could take, the main responsibility for their own daily care. These approaches could be used far more widely and enthusiastically, such as by helping young people waiting in clinics to share their expertise and talk about the many ways they find of combining chronic problems with a fulfilling lifestyle.[28]

How many of the problems which people report to health professionals can actually be treated by nursing or medical care, and how many require social and political change if they are to be alleviated? Defining the latter as a health problem can create and increase the person's sense of inadequacy. Some cases of 'school phobia' are self-preserving attempts to avoid bullies in the playground, or verbal abuse from a teacher. The term 'truant' implies that the child is irresponsible and needs sorting out. However, it may be the school which needs sorting out with comprehensive anti-bullying programmes involving all the pupils and staff.[29]

Conclusion

People who at most times and places in the world would be respected as useful young adults leading fulfilling fairly independent lives are now expected to wait in the time-warp we call adolescence. The group is widely disparaged in terms which are no longer accepted for other groups, such as women or ethnic minorities. How can this promote health and wellbeing in any age group? To call someone 'adolescent' describes nothing accurate apart from the age range, and is like calling all old people 'geriatric'. One of the greatest fallacies in the story of adolescence is the notion that it is true, and

based on biological and scientific facts. The story bears little relation to reality, except when it becomes a self-fulfilling prophecy of
immaturity. It is liable to create and compound the morbidity
which it is supposed to alleviate. The story barely existed before the
twentieth century; do we need it for the twenty-first? Instead, we
could treat everyone with appropriate respect and care, whatever
their age group, as the chapter by Chris Baker (Chapter 6) illustrates, showing how a sensitive service for teenagers can be a model
for improving adult wards. Given the international rise in morbidity
rates among young people,[30] we have to look beyond individual
cases and subgroups, and also attend to their place in society and to
how social beliefs and behaviours relate to teenagers' sickness and
health. These questions need to be high on the research agenda for
adolescent medicine.

References

1. Aries P. *Centuries of Childhood*. Harmondsworth: Penguin, 1962.
2. Locke J. Quoted in Musgrove F. *Youth and Social Order*. London:
   Routledge, 1984: 51.
3. Findlay J. *Arnold of Rugby*, 1925 (quoting sermon from 1839). Cited in
   Musgrove F. *Youth and Social Order*. London: Routledge, 1984: 55.
4. Musgrove F. *Youth and Social Order*. London: Routledge, 1984: 49.
5. Hendrick H. Constructions and reconstructions of British childhood: an interpretive survey 1800 to the present. In: James A, Prout A
   (eds) *Constructing and Reconstructing Childhood*. Basingstoke: Falmer,
   1990.
6. Hall GS. *Adolescence: Its Psychology and its Relations to Physiology, Anthro-
   pology, Sociology, Sex, Crime, Religion and Education*. New York:
   Appleton, 1904: 493.
7. Mayall B. Trumpets over the range. Unpublished literature review.
   London: Institute of Education, 1989.
8. Dobash RP, Dobash RE. *The Imprisonment of Women*. Oxford:
   Blackwell, 1986: 113.
9. Burt C. *The Young Delinquent*, 4th edition. Bickley: University of London Press, 1944.
10. Pailthorpe G. *Studies in Psychology of Delinquency*. Report from the
    Medical Research Council. London: HMSO, 1932.
11. Morrow V. Responsible children? Aspects of children's work and
    employment outside school in contemporary UK. In: Mayall B (ed)
    Children's Childhoods Observed and Experienced. London: Falmer, 1994:
    128–43.
12. Morss J. *The Biologising of Childhood: Developmental Psychology and the
    Darwinian Myth*. Hove: Lawrence Erlbaum Associates, 1990.
13. Macfarlane A. *The Psychology of Childbirth*. Edinburgh: Fontana, 1977.
14. Donaldson M. *Children's Minds*. Glasgow: Fontana, 1978.
15. Dunn J. *The Beginnings of Social Understanding*. Oxford: Blackwell,
    1988.

16. Nilsen R. Preschool children's expressions in the matter of 'sweethearts'. In: Nielson H (ed) *Social Construction of Gender in Children's Worlds*. Oslo Universitetet, 1994.
17. Tizzard B, Hughes M. *Young Children Learning*. Glasgow: Fontana, 1984.
18. Alderson P. *Children's Consent to Surgery*. Buckingham: Open University Press, 1993.
19. Solberg A. Negotiating childhood. In: James A, Prout A (eds) *Constructing and Reconstructing Childhood*. Basingstoke: Falmer, 1990.
20. Siegal M. *Knowing Children: Experiments in Conversation and Cognition*. Hove: Lawrence Erlbaum Associates, 1991.
21. Blanchard P. *The Child and Society*. New York, London: Longmans, Green and Co., 1928.
22. Kurtz Z, Stanley G. Epidemiology. In: Harvey D, Miles M, Smyth D (eds) *Community Childhealth & Paediatrics*. Oxford: Butterworth-Heinemann, 1995: 14.
23. Mansfield K. Quoted in Report of the Committee on Child Health Services, *Fit for the Future*. London: HMSO, 1976: 1.
24. Phoenix A. *Young Mothers?* Cambridge: Polity Press, 1991.
25. Arline T. On teenage childbearing and neonatal mortality in the US. *Population and Development Review* 1987; **13**: 245, 253, 260–7.
26. Rhode DL. Adolescent pregnancy and public policy. *Political Science Quarterly* 1993–4; **108**(4): 635–69.
27. British Paediatric Association. *Position Statement: Campaign to End the Physical Punishment of Children in the Home*. London: BPA, 1994.
28. Singh R. Personal experience of diabetes. In: Alderson P (ed) *Diabetes, Choice and Control: Consent Conference Report No. 8*. London: Social Science Research Unit, 1995.
29. Tattum D (ed). *Understanding and Managing Bullying*. London: Heinemann, 1993.
30. Rutter M, Smith D (eds). *Psycho-social Disorders in Young People: Time Trends and Their Causes*. Chichester: Wiley, 1995.

3 | National research and development priorities in adolescent health

Aidan Macfarlane
Director, National Adolescent and Student Health Unit, Oxford

---

The National Health Service Research and Development (R&D) strategy was launched in 1991 to help create a research-based health service in which reliable and relevant information is used to make decisions on health policy, clinical practice and management of services. In order to identify R&D priorities, NHS activity is in the process of being reviewed by the Central Research and Development Committee (CRDC) from six perspectives: disease-related problems; management and organisational issues; problems related to specific client groups; consumer issues; health technologies; and research methodologies.

Within these perspectives, time-limited expert advisory groups were convened to consider key areas in detail.

Physical and complex disability were subject to a CRDC review in 1993. Maternal and child health was the second review and took place in 1994.

An advisory group chaired by Professor Aynsley Green was set up in January 1994 to identify the R&D priorities for the NHS, relevant to mother and child health. The advisory group first met in March 1994 and formed three panels to focus on particular areas. These three panels covered:

- mother and infant health (up to one year),
- the health of the young child and its carers (one to ten years),
- the health of the older child/adolescent and its carers (ten to twenty years).

This chapter will only cover the work of the third panel. Its task was to identify R&D priorities for the NHS in relation to the health and health care needs of the older child and adolescent and its carers, including:

- health problems directly affecting this age group,

- behaviours in children and adolescents and aspects of the social environment which influence immediate and adult health (eg sexual behaviour, smoking, drug use etc.).

The panel was asked to recommend to the main Advisory Group on Mother and Child Health an ordered list of 10–15 topics relating to the older child and adolescents which would then be considered in competition with other recommendations from the other two panels. An overall priority list would then be recommended for inclusion for the national programme.

Method of working

Identifying research needs

Several different methods of working were used by the panel:

1. The panel members were asked to provide a list of research priorities that they would offer on the basis of the present knowledge. These were kept unread, till the end of the consultation process.
2. The panel members were asked to consider a number of available documents including specially commissioned papers.
3. The main source of evidence was through a process of consultation by which evidence was collected from a wide range of bodies within the NHS, from academic networks, from professional organisations, from consumer groups and others. Respondents were asked to suggest three problems or opportunities for research. In all, over 600 suggestions were received and considered by the panels.
4. Evidence was also taken from a seminar organised with Department of Health staff to ensure an input by policy-makers.
5. A workshop was set up to include participants from a number of backgrounds including adolescents themselves. Unfortunately this was cancelled owing to a rail strike so participants were asked to contribute on paper only.

Reviewing the material

Material from the postal consultation was summarised into one line abstracts and grouped by the secretariat at the Management Executive. It was then circulated to all members of the panel with a scoring sheet. Members were also provided with the original documentation to refer to where necessary.

Each item was rated against three criteria which had been discussed and agreed at the first panel meeting:

- the burden of the disease in terms of mortality and morbidity,
- the cost to society in terms of the provision of services provided and the cost to the patients themselves,
- the likely impact of research in terms of feasibility and implementability.

Taking these factors into account each suggestion was scored on a 9 point scale:

1	interesting (but not essential)
2–3	worthwhile (if resources permitted)
4–5	important to the NHS
6–7	of major importance to the NHS
8–9	of crucial importance to the NHS

Prioritising

From the scoring by members of the panel, a draft master list was drawn up. The panel then met to discuss the master list and to use an interactive electronic, blind, voting system to score each item discussed. This highlighted areas of high and low agreement using bimodal scores.

Ten top priorities and five further lower-order priorities were identified. Panel members then prepared supporting statements for these areas of research. The list of priorities and supporting statements were then submitted to the main advisory group.

General principles arising from the panel's discussion

1. The panel recognised that socioeconomic, political and environmental factors had a great influence on the health of young people and that these factors should form an integral part of any research agenda for the NHS. Therefore those commissioning research should consider the social dimension where relevant.
2. There were areas of research which were of crucial interest to the NHS but where major work was already being undertaken, eg long-term outcomes of children with cancer, and the aetiology and environmental factors associated with asthma.
3. Young people themselves should be consulted on the value of research undertaken.
4. Where routine data are collected, these should be in appropriate age groups to reflect the particular needs of older children and adolescents.

5. Services need to be accessible and appropriate to all young people, including those in particular groups (eg ethnic minorities and homeless young adults).

The priorities from the panel

1. The development of a routine minimum data set broken down into appropriate age groups to include (a) accidents and injuries, (b) occupational injuries, (c) acute morbidity data, especially relating to health care, (d) known risk factors affecting adverse health outcomes, and (e) the epidemiology of impairment, disability and handicap, including learning disabilities.
2. Identifying the views and needs of young people for health care services.
3. The cost-effectiveness of various strategies to prevent the onset of smoking.
4. The appropriate delivery of adolescent services; especially services in primary health care.
5. The effectiveness of interventions for young people with health problems.
6. Young people's views of interventions to change behaviours (smoking, drug taking etc).
7. The effectiveness of services to prevent disabilities from becoming handicaps.
8. Evaluation of health services for disabled young people and their carers.
9. Role of alcohol and drugs in injuries for young people.
10. Appropriateness of health/health care information given to young people and their carers.

Other priorities

• Identifying appropriate outcome measures for adolescents and their families for serious and/or disabling childhood conditions.
• Evaluation of primary health care/community interventions in reducing teenage pregnancies.
• Cost-effectiveness of interventions to prevent accidents.
• Burden on carers and society of the consequences of early medical interventions, eg intensive care.
• Long-term outcomes of disease processes and their treatment in children and young people including treatment for asthma, epilepsy and diabetes.

Panel members then considered their own original suggestions which showed considerable congruence to the final recommended list. The degree of congruity suggested that the overall exercise of consultation, although necessary from a political viewpoint, might possibly have been forshortened and still end up with the same results.

The priority list resulting from the panel's discussions was then discussed by the advisory group alongside the priorities submitted by the other two panels on (1) mother and infant health (up to one year), (2) the health of the young child and its carers (one to ten years). A new priority list was achieved by again using anonymous electronic voting.

The final overall list of R&D priorities recommended by the main advisory group covering all ages is shown in Table 1.

Table 1. R & D priorities for mother and child health recommended by the main advisory group

- Evaluation of different models of maternity care
- Interventions during labour: short- and long-term outcomes
- Mental and physical health of mother after birth and the impact on the family
- Evaluation of genetic services, to include access to, and delivery of, services; methods of education of professional staff and families; and evaluation of counselling and support for bereaved families
- Examination of causes, prevention, management and long-term outcome of babies born too early or too small
- Evaluation of the reasons for variation in outcome in the management of 'high-risk' neonates
- Impact of maternal and infant nutrition (including breast-feeding) on health and development
- Identifying interventions, including development of parenting skills, to reduce harmful effects of social and physical environment on health and development of mother and child
- Investigation and management of common infant problems, eg night waking, crying
- Evaluation of the effectiveness and cost of intervention to prevent injury, including an evaluation of the impact of such interventions on the quality of life of children, adolescents and their families
- Evaluation of the effectiveness and cost of the services provided for acutely injured children and adolescents
- Development of routine methods for the measurement of the age-related prevalence of disability and the development of appropriate outcome measures for evaluation of the services provided for infants, children, adolescents and their families with serious and/or disabling conditions
- Development and evaluation of methods to identify, correctly

Table 1. *continued*

> diagnose and provide for the needs of children and adolescents with complex disabilities and their families—with reference to models for the coordination of services within and between the health, social services and education sectors

- Development and evaluation of methods of providing information to parents, children and adolescents with complex disabilities to allow effective use of services
- Development and evaluation of guidelines for the appropriate skill mix and settings for the treatment of important common chronic illness in childhood and adolescence, eg diabetes, recurrent acute lower respiratory tract illness (including asthma), epilepsy, orthopaedic problems, mental health problems
- Development and evaluation of methods to inform and empower parents, children, adolescents and school teachers to undertake the everyday management of important chronic childhood illness, eg asthma, epilepsy, diabetes
- Evaluation of the cost and effectiveness of the current different models of service delivery for children and adolescents with emotional, behavioural or learning disorders
- Evaluation of strategies to change health behaviours in children and adolescents, eg smoking, drugs, unwanted pregnancies
- Identifying the needs and views of young people on the appropriate delivery of adolescent services, especially primary health care services
- Population-based evaluation of the ease of access to and the use of health care services by children in need, in particular those from materially disadvantaged families and minority ethnic groups
- Paediatric pharmacology: the safety and efficacy of drugs and the evaluation of drug use for infants

Taking the priorities forward

Following approval by the CRDC the final report of the advisory group was circulated widely as a policy document.

Responsibility for ensuring that the priorities were planned, in process or commissioned by the NHS was the responsibility of the Programme Director of the Child Health Programme—Professor Terry Stacey—and a Programme Management Team (PMT).

The work of the PMT involves (a) achieving an understanding of work already going on, and (b) liaising and coordination between regional health authorities' research portfolios, the Department's own centrally commissioned programme of R&D and funded institutions such as the Cochrane Centre and the Centre for Reviews and Dissemination. Where work is neither planned nor in progress the work is commissioned through the NHS R&D programme.

A rider from the final overall draft report (prepared by Professor Aynsley Green) of the CRDC Advisory Group Identifying R&D Priorities for the NHS in Mother and Child Health

> These priorities are not definitive or absolute. They represent the consensus view of one group of experts on the pressing research needs on mother and child health at this moment in time. Priorities will change as new evidence emerges as the service itself changes over the coming years. These priorities should be reviewed in two or three years time and the impact of the report and the resulting research activity should be evaluated.

Acknowledgement

This chapter is a summary of the enormous amount of hard work done by Tara Lamont, working in the secretariat to support the R&D initiative at the NHS Executive Headquarters in Leeds. I am deeply grateful to her for all that she has done to make this possible and for all her support during the course of the panel meetings. I am also extremely grateful to Professor Aynsley Green for permission to reproduce this material.

PART TWO

Services for adolescents—
what should they be?

4 | Primary health care and adolescence

Ann McPherson
General practitioner, Oxford

In spite of the evidence that adolescents visit their GPs two or three times a year,[1] the primary health care services have largely ignored the specific needs of this age group. This is partly because until recently there has been little information available about what adolescents, aged between 10 and 18, want from the primary health care services or what adolescent health needs are that can be supplied by the primary health care services.[2]

There is now a flurry of activity in the area. The Department of Health has had its own initiative on 'The Health of the Young Nation'.[3] The Royal College of General Practitioners has set up its own working group on the subject, and now general practices are having to reflect on what they are doing for adolescents.

Because the primary health care team does see both young people *and* their parents on a regular basis, they do have a central role to play. However, it is only part of a much broader picture, involving governmental economic policies and educational and social policies.

General health of adolescents

Surveys of this age group show that around 70–90% consider themselves to be in 'excellent health'.[4,5] Nevertheless, nearly three-quarters had taken medicines in the previous 4 weeks (40% of this was for headaches), three-quarters actually suffered from headaches and three-quarters had fillings in their teeth. But, for the majority, their sense of 'overall quality' of life appears unaffected by these relatively minor inconveniences that intermittently affect us all and that we choose not to take significant notice of. It is therefore important not to overmedicalise the lives of adolescents but, at the same time, recognise that over three-quarters of adolescents see themselves as responsible for their own health, and three-quarters also understand that the way they choose to live will influence their own health.[4]

What adolescents attend primary care for

The common minor illnesses reported by adolescents themselves are coughs and colds (13%), hayfever (5%), skin problems (5%) and asthma (4%).[1] Over a third of adolescents have seen their GP in the previous 3 months.[4]

The commonest reasons for consulting are for minor injuries, including sports injuries, minor illnesses, and travel immunisations. Use of medicines and consultation rates seem to be clearly established at around 15 years of age with young males consulting less and taking fewer medicines than their female counterparts. For all problems young women consulted more than young men but this was much more marked for those labelled by GPs as 'trivial'. There is some evidence that teenagers are seen for a shorter consultation time than other patients.[6] This may be because of the type of problem being brought or because they are being short changed!

Adolescents' usual sources of health advice

When adolescents are asked whom they first turn to for advice on health problems, 86% say their parents. Parents are closely followed by friends and then television, books and magazines,[4] with *Just 17, More* and *Jackie* leading the field.

As adolescents get older, there is naturally a greater emphasis on the need for more 'independent' sources of information including learning from their peers and health professionals. Overall only 7% of 14–17 year olds gave doctors as their first source of medical advice.[1,4]

What adolescents want from their GP

Two studies show that many more adolescents (both male and female) would like to discuss health-related subjects—sexually transmitted diseases, contraception, nutrition, fears about cancer—with a health professional (GP, school doctor or nurse) than actually do.[2] Is this because health professionals are seen as 'curing disease' rather than offering advice? Is it difficulty over accessibility? Is it shyness on the part of the teenager? These questions still need answering and the results responded to accordingly.

What adolescents do and do not appreciate about present primary health care facilities

An attempt has been made to find out what teenagers do and do not want from primary care by administering a questionnaire to sixth formers. Out of 100 lower sixth formers (aged about 17) 30 answered the question 'Were there things that you especially liked about your local health centre?'. Half of them mentioned 'friend-liness'—'friendly doctor', 'friendly receptionist', 'friendly and helpful staff', 'friendly atmosphere'.

Out of the 40 respondents answering the question 'Were there things that you did not like about visiting the local health centre?' a quarter mentioned the quiet/silence—'very quiet in the waiting room', 'too morbid, sad and quiet', 'too quiet and stuffy'. The second most common complaint was 'too short with the doctor, too long waiting to get in', which may be a complaint shared by a rather wider age group.

What adolescents rate as important in primary health care facilities

A focus group of teenagers identified six areas of importance about services in general practice:

- having notices and magazines especially for young people in the waiting rooms,
- friendly and welcoming staff at the front desk,
- being able to phone up the practice and ask advice, if necessary without having to give your name,
- being absolutely sure that anything that you discuss with any member of the practice team (family doctor, nurses, reception etc.) will stay absolutely confidential and nothing will be said to anyone else (parents, teachers, etc.),
- having good written information available from the health centre about things like contraception, exercise, diet,
- having a clinic run at the health centre especially for young people aged 10–20.

A group of 188 teenagers were asked to 'list them in order', and the results of their responses are shown in Fig 1.

These results demonstrate that it is essential for practices to *positively* reassure teenagers that everything they communicate will be dealt with absolutely confidentially. Secondly, and also to do with confidentiality, is *making it possible* for the adolescent to phone in and get advice on a 'no name' basis. This might be difficult to

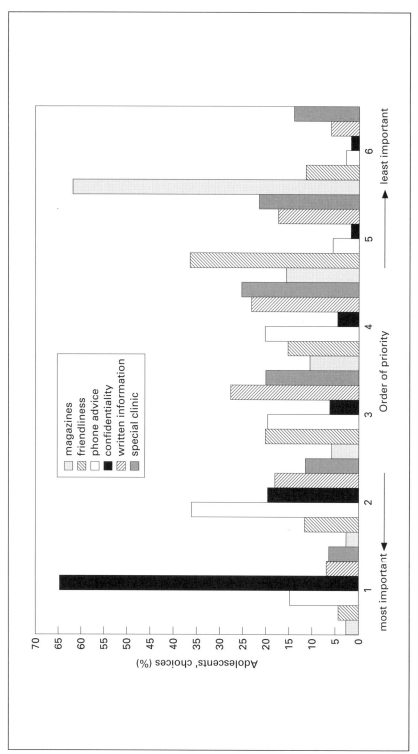

Fig 1. *Service provisions in primary health care ranked in order of importance by adolescents. (n = 188)*

deliver in practice but it should be possible to encourage receptionists to intimate to patients who are reluctant to give their name
that they can still get information.

Good written information comes third—and needs to be
reviewed. There are huge numbers of leaflets available to
teenagers on every health and illness subject. However, how many
of these leaflets have been field tested with adolescents themselves
to assess their readability, design, information content, appropriateness of subject etc? The National Adolescent and Student
Health Unit in Oxfordshire is involved in collecting as many available leaflets as possible to put before a panel of adolescent judges
to assess consumer satisfaction.

There were female/male differences which were most striking in
the answers about confidentiality, but which also showed that
males were more likely to want confidential phone advice, perhaps
reflecting their inability to talk to friends and others around them
about their concerns. The male/female difference as far as want-
ing magazines in the waiting room was concerned is probably due
to the fact that more girls already buy and read these themselves.

Priorities for change

There are many ways in which primary care can be improved for
young people but it is important to prioritise what and how it can
be done. The eight priorities listed give a framework to start the
process.

1. Identifying characteristics of the practice population 10–18 year olds. By
using the practice's 'age/sex register' and using a degree of common sense and people's knowledge, it is relatively easy to work out
a profile for the local population that falls in this age group. The
other suggestions for change outlined below may need to be
modified in the light of this profile.

2. Providing positive information about confidentiality. Adolescents are
used to the fact that much of what they say about themselves, the
way they behave and what they think, is not treated as confidential
but is the subject of extensive discussion by peers, family, teachers
etc. Contact with primary health care teams may be the first time
that the concept of absolute confidentiality will have been mooted.
It is therefore essential for practices to put out a positive message
about absolute confidentiality via posters, leaflets, reassurance during face-to-face consultations and that this applies to *every* member
of the practice.

3. Making the practice more adolescent user friendly. A priority should be to make sure that GPs themselves, practice nurses and the receptionists are user friendly to *adolescents* (not always easy to achieve). The positive comments about 'friendliness' above, and adverse comments like 'doctors not friendly, know my parents but . . .' and 'unfriendly attitudes of receptionist' clearly indicate the need for special sensitivity, thought, training (including role playing and videotaping) and action in this area of provision. Other easy areas to change are (a) the kind of posters on the walls of waiting rooms—are there any directed at adolescents? (b) leaflets—are there ones suitable for this age group? (c) magazines—are there any in the waiting rooms suitable for this age group?

One further practical measure, which has been patchily used, is arranging for fifth and sixth formers to visit the practice as part of their *school* 'personal development' programme.

4. Offering freedom to change GPs at the age of 16. Teenagers need to know that they can go to other doctors particularly, if they want, one not responsible for the care of their parents, and they need also to be positively assured that doctors themselves will not be offended by this.

5. Routine checks at 16 years of age may be one way of helping to contact adolescents. There is some research to support this concept. In one study[7] when 13, 15 and 17 year olds were invited for a general practice health check, 73% attended with a similar response rate in men and women. In a separate study,[8] also in London, calling the practice's 16 year olds in for a health check, only 50% responded. Further evaluation of other such initiatives still needs to be undertaken before fully recommending them because it is all too easy to retreat into the familiar medical model used for older age groups, and which may well be totally inappropriate for this age group. Much more important may be concentrating on informing adolescents about what health services are supplied by the primary health care team and the confidentiality issue.

6. Specific clinics for teenagers. These are beginning to be set up by many practices all over the UK. Their effectiveness is unevaluated, though there is evidence from other countries where they have been run for some time that they can be well used and appreciated. From the survey we undertook (see Fig 1), such clinics do not rate high with adolescents themselves and most such clinics have found that, at least initially, attendance is very low. A more successful alternative may be for various practices to encourage the development of a local community clinic run by the community services in areas of high need (high unemployment, inner city areas, lack of other facilities, etc.).

7. Specific help and information for parents to help them in their role as primary carer of their children. During most of the teenage years, parents continue to be the main providers, carers and sources of information. This role could be more fully recognised by those providing primary health care. Drug information, how to put over contraceptive advice in general and emergency contraception information in particular, signs of when a child is depressed, how to deal with 'acting out behaviour' are all areas in which information provision for parents could be evaluated. With the rapidly developing role of community nursing within primary health care and the Health of the Nation targets relative to this age group (smoking, alcohol, diet, pregnancy, suicide etc.), GPs and nurses could look at extending their roles with the under fives into the older age group via the parents.

8. Training in primary health care. GP registrars have weekly training sessions which need to include specific training in 'adolescent health'. A training pack is now available[9] for registrars in general practice which includes an adolescent audit and practice profile, background reading papers giving the facts on adolescent health, examples of critical reading, ideas for role play etc. so that all new GPs should have had some training specifically in the discipline. Hopefully, there will be a 'trickle down effect' into the practices via the GP registrars.

Role of primary health care teams (PHCTs) in health promotion to adolescents

Much of the work to be done in this area will be tied in with the 'Health of the Nation' targets.[10] The ones that are specifically relevant are:

- Cutting the smoking rate of 11–15 year olds by 33%—from 8% in 1988 to 6% (60% of adult smokers started before the age of 16). The main PHCT input is helping teenagers who are smoking to give up.
- Cutting the calories from fat from 40% to below 35% of total calorie intake (eating habits are embedded even as far back as the womb with the results of high cholesterol being laid down in the coronary arteries from an early age). It could be argued that there is a role for PHCTs in providing information on an

opportunistic basis, but accepting that advice in this area not only changes over time, but also from one professional group to another.

- Cutting deaths due to accidents in the 15–24 age group by 25% from 23.2 per 100,000 to no more than 17.4 (the major cause of death in young people). The role of PHCTs here is uncertain as most deaths in this age group are male and are due to road traffic accidents. Opportunistically there may be a limited role for PHCTs, on cycle helmet wearing.
- Cutting the pregnancy rate in under 16s by 50%—from 9.5 per 1,000 girls aged 13–15 in 1989 to no more than 4.8 (pregnancy during the teens has a higher rate of prematurity and there are also a wide range of socioeconomic consequences). Here there is a definite role for the PHCT in provision of contraceptive advice and user friendliness in providing emergency contraception.
- Cutting the overall suicide rate by 15%—from 11.1 per 100,000 population in 1990 to no more than 9.4 (there is a steady rise in male adolescent suicides at the present time). There is a possible role here for PHCTs in recognising depression in young people, but this will need both training and evaluation.

The major initiative for achieving most of these health targets has to come from the government. Whilst the government continues policies that allow social inequalities to get greater, and refuses to ban advertising on smoking, enact legislation concerning cycle helmet wearing, or force manufacturers to be more open about food contents, it is difficult to take these targets, or the government, seriously.

Conclusion

Much can be done to improve facilities for adolescents attending primary health care. In many cases, little is needed in the way of resources other than a short hard input to make a few key changes in normal practice life. A small amount of extra appropriate information about confidentiality and services, and a little extra thought and friendliness are the most essential elements needed.

References

1. Balding J. *Young people in 1988.* HEA Schools Health Education Unit. Higher Hoopern Farm, University of Exeter, Exeter EX4 4QJ.

2. Epstein R, Rice P, Wallace P. Teenagers' health concerns: implications for primary health care professionals. *Journal of the Royal College of General Practitioners* 1989; **39**: 247–9.

3. *Health of the Young Nation.* 1995, London: HMSO.

4. Macfarlane A, *et al.* Teenagers and their health. *Archives of Disease in Childhood* 1987; **62**: 1125–9.

5. Challener J. Health education in secondary schools—is it working? A study of 1,418 Cambridgeshire pupils. *Public Health* 1990; **104**: 195–205.

6. Jacobson LD, *et al.* Is the potential of teenage consultations being missed?: a study of consultation times in primary care. *Family Practice* 1994; 269–99.

7. Townsend J, *et al.* Adolescent smokers seen in general practice: health, lifestyle, physical measurements, and response to anti-smoking advice. *British Medical Journal* 1991; **303**: 947–50.

8. Donovan CF, McCarthy S. Is there a place for adolescent screening in general practice. *Health Trends* 1988; **2**: 20; 64.

9. Adolescent Health—A Training Pack for Trainees in General Practice. National Adolescent and Student Health Unit in Association with the RCGP, 1995.

10. Department of Health. *Health of the Nation.* London: HMSO.

5 | Community services for the school age child

Leon Polnay
Reader in Child Health, University of Nottingham

Historical background

School health services were first established universally in 1907 after the report of the Interdepartmental Committee on Physical Deterioration. This report was commissioned because of the high rate of rejection of recruits for the Boer War. Some of its recommendations, listed in Table 1, showed great insight and indeed many similarities to our current Health of the Nation targets.

Table 1. 1904 Report of the Interdepartmental Committee on Physical Deterioration[1]

- problems not new
- reports not new
- among their 53 recommendations
  - anthropometric survey—on-going programme of measurement of child growth
  - overcrowding—a standard to be established and enforced
  - buildings and open spaces—compulsory preservation of open spaces in building regulations
  - air pollution—higher penalties for pollution and stricter enforcement
  - alcoholism—instruction in schools on health hazards
  - juvenile smoking—prohibit sale of tobacco to children
  - food and cooking—training in schools
  - adulteration of foods—standard purity for food and drinks
  - physical exercise—methodical physical exercise in schools
  - medical inspection of school children—public duty for systematic medical inspection
  - investigate the extent and character of lunacy in Ireland

Indeed school health services date back into the last century and the quotation below from Newsholme's School Hygiene,[2] first published in 1887, indicates some concerns, which until recently would be uncomfortably familiar.

43

The work of medical inspectors of schools largely consists in filling up answers to the numerous questions on these schedules and completing forms for treatment, re-examination, and other objects arising out of them. There is little time for careful observation, and insufficient time to form a clear picture of each child as a whole, so that the doctor soon resigns himself to noting the isolated signs on cards.

High quality information was available on the service and three examples from 1913 illustrate this very well. It is doubtful if this type of information is routinely available anywhere in the UK at the present time.

Example 1: Weight of boys age 5, Nottingham, 1913[3]

Better class school	$n = 167$	Average weight 18.45 kg
Medium class school	$n = 809$	Average weight 17.73 kg
Poorer class school	$n = 243$	Average weight 15.66 kg
Standard		18.09 kg

Example 2: Visual acuity of school leavers, boys, Nottingham, 1913[3]

1,750	tested
1	not tested
30	squint

All classified in a table of VA right versus VA left, eg

VA 6/6 6/6	954
VA 6/60 6/60	5

Example 3: Referrals for defective vision, Nottingham, 1913[3]

Number referred	1,293
Number not responding	815
had private examination and glasses prescribed	133
had private examination and did not need glasses	51
left school	243
no steps taken	388
Number who did reply to letter	478
granted free examination	465
number attended	415
free examination and glasses	197
free examination and glasses on instalment plan	147

328 pairs of glasses prescribed at 1s 5d
cost (less parental contribution)
    = £12 7s 7d

Although services have changed considerably since this time, there is still much which we could learn from this example.

For some time in the early and middle part of this century there was a progressive narrowing of the service into school medical inspections and special education medical examinations. Great expertise in this area was achieved, but much progress was outside of the conventional mainstream of paediatrics. At the same time hospital paediatrics and general practice were expanding rapidly. A turning point was the publication of the Court Report in 1976.[4] This contained a clear and comprehensive vision for child health services in the community. Following on from it were a wide range of developments including consultant appointments, training programmes, unification with the main body of paediatrics, academic expansion and a widening of the range of services provided.

Current services

This chapter summarises the current services under the headings of 14 separate programmes of care. They are based upon the Report of the Joint BPA Working Party, *Health Needs of School Age Children* (1995).[5]

The report divides services into two groups:

Services for all children

- Health promotion
- Accident prevention
- Core programme for child health surveillance
- Dental health
- Infectious disease control and immunisation
- Adolescent health

Services for children in need

Social issues	*Disability*
● Child protection	● Developmental problems
● Children 'looked after'	● Emotional and behavioural problems
● Adoption and fostering	● Ill health (general paediatrics)
● Disadvantage	● Critical illness

These cannot be described here other than in outline. However, there are many common principles behind these programmes and these will now be described in more detail.

Collaboration

The school health services lie at the crossroads between health, education and social services. Originally, they formed part of the local authority and today a very high level of cooperation is required between these agencies. Within health care, the term *seamless* is often used, but this should also be applied to 'networking' with education and social services. The first set of seams apply to the various age groups—pre-school to primary, primary to secondary, secondary to adolescent and adolescent to adult. There should be a smooth transition across all of these boundaries—this is far from being always the case. The second set of seams apply to the different places or settings where children and young people may be seen: these are the home, school, clinic, GP surgery and hospital. These may provide a single integrated service to an individual, but in other cases, communication and cooperation is poor. Child protection is particularly problematic where the need for this occurs. The third set of seams comprise the people who staff health, education and social services. They serve the same population and yet in the worst circumstances might not even know one another's names never mind work together. The fourth set of seams is about the purpose of the components of the service, for example prevention, case finding and management. The example from 1913 is a good illustration of the broad overview required of all aspects of the service. The fifth set of seams refers to 'pounds' in terms of delineating the responsibility of individual budget holders. As budgets become tighter, there is an attempt to redefine the provision that it is intended to cover and disputes, sometimes called the 'it's not my budget syndrome' can lead to long delays in children receiving the services that they need.

Another aspect of collaboration is partnership with parents and young people. This is encouraged by developments such as the personal child health record, the recognition of the importance of children's rights enshrined in the UN Charter[6] and the desirability of the service to consult with young people, to accept self-referrals and respect confidentiality.

A group of people and agencies working together may be described as a *consortium*. For example, for hearing problems this consortium will involve neonatal screening in the maternity unit, screening by the primary health care team, referral to a specialist hearing assessment centre, an ear, nose and throat service, specialist education services and a social work team.

Information

The importance of information was well known to our predecessors in 1913 and their data were collected without the aid of computers. Today we collect information, but retrieval and use is often problematic. We have strongly recommended that the information should be related to individual localities, based upon the size of area that might contain a 'family' of schools. These locality profiles should be used to compile an annual report for the governors of each school on the health and health needs of their pupils. The annual report would contain information about the individual school compiled by the health workers responsible. The information requires interpretation and should lead to recommendations to the school and community health services. The report would be copied to the Director of Public Health. It is hoped that this will not only enable individual children's health needs to be met, but also provide a broad overview of the health of the school population as a whole, with an opportunity to influence the policies of schools and the purchasers of health services.

Critical mass

We have not given any precise staffing levels for each of the programmes of care. Where these are described in detail through local clinical guidelines and manuals of practice and where the number of individuals enrolled in each programme is known, staffing levels can be calculated. The Audit Commission, in its report *Seen but not heard*,[7] described quite wide variation in staffing levels between districts. Some of this may be explained by some providing a much broader range of services in the community than others, for example more general paediatric clinics as an alternative to hospital outpatients. However, others, even in the presence of an appropriate clinical guideline, do not have a sufficient critical mass of staffing to deliver it effectively. If services are ineffective, they are vulnerable to the critical eye of the purchaser. Services such as those for children with emotional and behavioural problems are often very time intensive, but appointments at six monthly intervals are not very effective. In child protection, the service can consist of notification only, notification plus initial assessment and report, notification plus assessment and report plus attendance at case conference, or notification plus assessment and report plus case conference attendance with follow-up appointments, for example with regard to behavioural management, family relationships or for the victims of sexual abuse. The staff levels and skill mix required for each of these options is obviously quite different; which level of service provides the most effective programme of care should be quite obvious. Some districts do not get beyond stage one. With the current emphasis on health promotion, programmes that are extremely thin, even if the principles are sound, are unlikely to be effective. A consistent and continuing health promotion message throughout the school years is needed, but based on evidence of effectiveness.

Access

Access to the service is required by many routes. For a surgeon repairing hernias, access via the GP can be accepted as the single pathway. For health services for school age children, the picture is not as simple. Education and social services do require advice and there are statutory obligations to provide it (eg Education Act 1993). Individual pupils may also wish to self-refer to the school nurse or doctor and may also request confidentiality. There are seldom problems in this more complex situation, with multiple points of entry into the network, provided that there is good communication, local services work together and local service agreements are developed.

Continuity of care

'Best buy' programmes (those that make optimal use of skill mix and staff rotas) often do not receive strong approval by parents and young people because some deliver a service that is fragmented between practitioners within an individual organisation. This may be because of high staff turnover, because trainees are attached for short periods only or for other operational reasons, such as time off duty or scheduling of clinics. For children and young people with long-term and complex special needs, continuity is especially important, not only with the family, but also within the professional network.

Identified lead responsibility

Whilst an individual paediatrician working in a locality is the lead person for that locality, each programme of care requires a lead responsibility at district level. For some such as the immunisation coordinator or the child protection coordinator, guidelines are already laid down, but in the latter case, not all districts have identified such posts. Other lead roles are being defined, such as the district child health surveillance coordinator, a lead role for children 'looked after' or for adolescent services. Lead responsibility includes a responsibility for strategy and planning, for compiling information about the service and its delivery and for being the focal point for communication.

Advocacy

The service, whilst being able to identify and refer individual children in need as well as influencing policy through reports to school governors and directors of public health, often finds itself in the position of advocate. Liaison paediatrics can involve a coordinating role between several individuals and agencies involved and add weight to ensure that promised programmes of care actually are delivered. This is a common position with children with long-term special needs and for children who are disadvantaged. This has for a long time been a role taken by community services and it remains an important one.

Individual programmes of care

Health promotion

Health promotion is included in that national curriculum and has been focused within the health service by means of *Health of the Nation*[8] targets. The work of school nurses is changing by moving towards health promotion, both on an individual basis and through support to schools in their delivery of the national curriculum. Local information, for example on accidents, obesity, pregnancy rates, will help to target limited resources/services. Special issues may be encouraging schools in areas such as healthy eating or anti-bullying campaigns.

Accident prevention

Accidents remain the commonest cause of death among school age children and reduction of deaths from accidents is an important *Health of the Nation*[8] target. A multidisciplinary Local Child Accident Prevention Committee should be established in every district to coordinate policy and planning. Paediatricians have a key role to play in these groups.

Core programme

As our knowledge has expanded, and as the pattern of morbidity changes in childhood, the number of medical checks of all children by doctors has been reduced from checks at 5, 7, 11 and 14 to, in most districts, selective referral of school entrants by the school nurse. The detailed programme, published in *Health Needs of School Age Children*,[5] consists of school nurse interviews at 5, 7–8, 11–12 and at 14 and monitoring of growth, vision and hearing. An increasing proportion of the health interview may be taken up by health promotion. As for the other programmes of care, intended for all children, it is important to ensure that the uptake is high. In 1913, only one school leaver missed the test of visual acuity!

Adolescent health

Adolescent health is the topic of this volume and one of great concern to the Working Party on Health Needs of School Age Children, with evidence of a decrease in some health measures being reported and a large amount of unmet need. We placed emphasis on consultation with young people in service planning and the need to provide a customised service that is different from that for adults or younger children. The elements of such a service include a central 'drop in' clinic, health monitoring at school, easy access to information, and a service for young people with disabilities. Homelessness among adolescents is increasing. Programmes of care need to be developed to reach this particularly disadvantaged group of young people.

Disability

Services for children with disabilities often present a series of complex needs and require large and diverse service networks to meet these needs. It is an area where community services have excelled and now have to meet new challenges. With improved survival of very low birth weight babies, more children with cerebral palsy are entering into the education system. There is also a continuing trend to switch from special school provision to provision in mainstream schools. The overall need is increased for medical, nursing and therapy services and these may have to be delivered in a more flexible manner. Another seamless service should be the Child Development Centre with outreach into schools and the community. A special needs register is required for individual management and service planning. Community paediatricians will be involved with special needs coordinators in schools in the staged assessment of children with special educational needs under the new 1993 Education Act.[9] A process of planning, review and monitoring should take place throughout the school years.

Emotional and behavioural difficulties

These form the largest cause of disability among children of school age. Important areas are bullying and its consequences, children who are excluded from school, the rising suicide rate in young men, the consequences of child sexual abuse and challenging behaviour in children with severe learning difficulties. Whilst some of these children may be seen by child and adolescent psychiatrists, behaviour problems still form up to 40% of the workload of the community paediatrician. These children are also of major concern to teachers, social workers and police. It follows, therefore, as for many other community services, that close local collaboration in planning and service delivery is essential. The service includes not only early identification and intervention, but also mental health promotion. School policies to combat bullying and promote self-esteem are important measures.

General paediatrics

Much general paediatrics currently provided from outpatient clinics can also be provided in the community through hospital outreach, by community paediatricians or through a combined child health service. Clinics provided nearer to home mean less disruption to school and a service that is easier to relate to local schools and local primary health teams.

Child protection

Child protection has already been referred to under some of the general principles underlying programmes of care. Quality standards for this service are being improved and a comprehensive and specialist service is expected.

Children 'looked after'

These must form the most needy group of children in the population. They have high rates of school non-attendance, learning difficulties, emotional and behavioural problems including self-harm, child prostitution and teenage pregnancy. They often have fragmented health care and outcomes in adult life are poor. Attempts are now being made to establish paediatricians as link doctors for community homes and to provide a comprehensive assessment of health, mental health and health promotion needs to inform their health care plan. Parallel to this residential social workers and foster parents need information, advice and support if all these health care needs are to be met.

Disadvantaged children

These are sadly a growing proportion of children of school age. With the support of the 1989 Children Act,[10] there is a duty to identify and refer children in need. The association with poorer health is well established. Local information should include numbers of homeless families, traveller families, those in poor housing, those living in poverty and families with overwhelming difficulties. Many districts still do not target their services and indeed some have lower levels of staffing in their more deprived areas because of unfilled vacancies or inflexibility in the allocation of resources. Only recently have the problems of young carers been recognised. There are also young people who are looking after an adult with physical or mental health problems. They are frequently 'invisible' to the professional health workers and may be reluctant to seek help because they do not know how to access it or they fear being taken into care if they think others perceive them as not coping. Specialist support services for young carers such as that in Nottingham are just developing.

This chapter has provided a brief summary of current community services for children of school age, with glances into the past. A glance into the future shows a great potential for growth and development. The merits and achievements of this service should be acknowledged more widely and investment made for the future of school age children in adult life.

References

1. Report of the Interdepartmental Committee on Physical Deterioration, 1904.
2. Kerr J. *Newsholme's School Hygiene: The Laws of Health in Relation to School Life*. New edition rewritten for all school health workers by James Kerr, MA MD. 14th edition. London: George Allen and Unwin, 1916.
3. School Medical Officer, Annual Report 1913, City of Nottingham Education Committee, 1914.
4. *Fit for the future*. Report of the Committee on Child Health Services

(Court Report). London: HMSO, Cmnd 6684, 1976.

5. British Paediatric Association. *Health Needs of School Age Children.* Report of the Joint Working Party, 1995.

6. United Nations. *Convention on the rights of the child.* Treaty Series 44, London: HMSO, 1992.

7. Audit Commission. *Seen but Not Heard.* London: HMSO, 1994.

8. Department of Health. *Health of the Nation—a Strategy for Health in England.* London: HMSO, 1992.

9. Education Act 1993, Code of Practice, DFE, 1994.

10. Children Act. London: HMSO, 1989.

6 | Developing a service for adolescents in a district general hospital

Christine Baker
Senior Nurse, Royal Gwent Hospital, Newport

The Platt report[1] was clear in its recommendations that adolescents should not be nursed in adult wards. Adolescents need their own accommodation but if the numbers do not warrant this then it is better for them to be nursed with children than with adults. The Court report[2] identified that adolescents require special attention and that they warrant consideration as a distinct group for health provision. Despite many other reports since then it appears that this distinctive group are still not being recognised by health professionals as a whole.

Need for a young persons ward

In 1987 a report by the Committee on the Welfare of Children in Hospital[3] highlighted results of a survey undertaken in 1984, which confirmed that a large proportion of adolescents were being nursed with adults. This report identified acceptable standards, one of which actually questions if the needs of adolescents have ever been reviewed. The report prompted great interest and concerns within our paediatric department at the Royal Gwent Hospital. We knew that some adolescents were being cared for on adult wards but statistics were not readily available. It was therefore decided to undertake a survey of where children and adolescents were being nursed within our hospital and this commenced in January 1988 for one year. What was uncovered was a shock to everyone concerned (Fig 1). Nine hundred and sixty 11–16 year olds were identified as having been cared for on adult wards, as were a further 70 children aged 0–10 years. Naturally grave concerns were voiced. From this audit it was realised that the rights of the child and adolescent were being greatly abused, and that adolescents as a distinct consumer group were not being recognised.

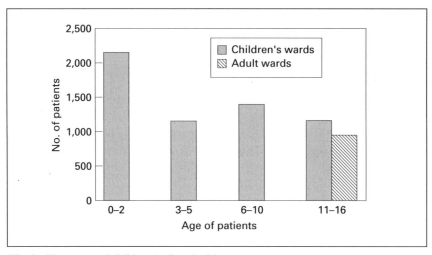

Fig 1. *Placement of children in hospital by age*

Armed with these figures we established the need for a young persons ward which would nurse all specialties including general medicine. Many documents were used to support the proposal, such as NAWCH (National Association for the Welfare of Children in Hospital) standards for adolescents,[4] *The Health of Youth*,[5] Platt,[1] Court,[2] the British Paediatric Association,[6] and many others. More importantly we questioned our consumer group, particularly the large number of adolescent cystic fibrosis patients. It was quite evident there was an urgent need for a young persons ward within the Royal Gwent Hospital and that it should be linked with the paediatric unit.

To achieve this meant lengthy negotiations with management and other disciplines. It is well documented that those districts that have established separate provision for adolescents have found it cost-effective, and most importantly it frees adult beds which are constantly under extreme pressure.[4,7]

Approval was eventually given for the young persons ward. We were particularly fortunate as a new 'purpose built' children's unit was being planned at this time, which meant simply reorganising the allocation of wards and age groups. The young persons ward was allocated 19 beds. It was felt that this would be an appropriate number since the population of South Gwent is approximately 300,000 and, as estimated by the British Paediatric Association,[6] each district general hospital (DGH) serving a population of approximately 200,000 would require a minimum of 15 adolescent beds.

Children and Young Persons Unit

The demands and needs of the adolescent/teenager require particular nursing skills and perhaps an even greater degree of sensitivity than is normally required by children and adults. This was being fully acknowledged by the nursing and medical staff of the paediatric unit. In April 1991 the new Children and Young Persons Unit opened. The young persons ward is situated on the seventh floor of the DGH and has been aptly nicknamed 'The Penthouse Suite'. Although attached to the paediatric unit the ward is self-contained and caters for patients aged 11–19 years from all specialties. It was decided to extend the age group so that teenagers between the ages of 17 and 19 years were also given the opportunity to use these facilities, and more importantly, it allows easier transfer of long-term patients to other specialties, such as general medicine. The ward, which is extremely popular, has excellent facilities for teenagers. It comprises (Fig 2) three 4 bedded bays, and seven single rooms, four of which have en suite facilities. Two of the single rooms can cater for total isolation with positive and negative ventilation. During the process of furnishing the ward views and thoughts were obtained from our patients; the result is that the decor is very suitable for the adolescent/teenager. Each bed has a Parker Knoll recliner which allows a parent to be resident if they so wish. Guidance on parental accommodation for the age group 12–16 years was obtained from a report published in 1986 by Caring for Children in the Health Service[8] in which they recommend 25% bed availability for a resident parent. There are toilet and washing facilities for patients and parents, and a refreshment area is also available. Recreational activities are well catered for, each bed has piped audio service, television and video, and we are extremely fortunate as a local video shop owner has adopted the ward and supplies films on a weekly basis free of charge. The most popular pieces of equipment used by the teenagers are the computers, although excellent use is also made of the snooker table and other facilities which are located in the leisure room. The hospital radio provides the teenagers with their own quiz/request programme.

We have enthusiastic play specialists who have arranged a number of activities such as discotheques and quiz nights. One of these was patients versus staff, and needless to say, the teenagers won.

Schooling is provided on a daily basis by our enthusiastic teacher who works five mornings per week. One of the great assets required in running a successful teenagers ward is to acknowledge

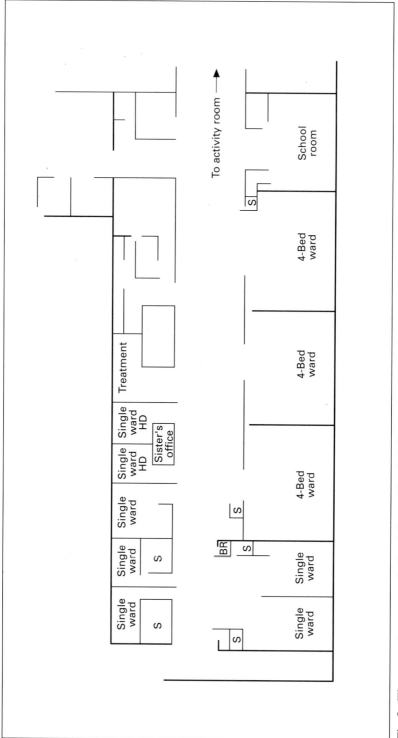

Fig 2. *The young persons ward, Royal Gwent Hospital* (S, service room, ie toilets, showers, storage cupboards. BR, beverage room. HD, high dependency)

young people's need for dignity and privacy, and a flexible approach is essential. At first it was difficult for staff in other departments to realise that the young persons ward was fully operational. However, they are now beginning to accept that teenage patients require and have special facilities.

It cannot be emphasised enough that ongoing communication and awareness raising is vital. A monthly audit report is produced which can identify which age groups continue to be admitted to adult wards. We are now able to state that 99% of young persons aged 16 years and below are being admitted to the Children and Young Persons Unit. The 1% admitted elsewhere are attending day surgery or require critical care. This is a drastic reduction compared with 1988.

There has been a constant increase in admissions: from April 1991 to April 1992 a total of 1,585 adolescents/teenagers were cared for on this 19 bedded ward. Most recent figures identify an increase to 1,823. Constant pressure is being applied to other health service staff to ensure that teenagers have a right to informed decisions on where they wish to be nursed. As displayed in Tables 1 and 2 there have been dramatic improvements. In relation to bed usage by specialty both general and orthopaedic surgery account for approximately 40% occupancy while paediatric and general medicine account for 38% with ENT and other specialties 22%. The average

Table 1. Monthly totals of admissions on young persons unit (YPU) and totals of young persons admitted to other wards (OW), April 1993 to March 1994

Month	15 yrs (OW)	15 yrs (YPU)	16 yrs (OW)	16 yrs (YPU)	17 yrs (OW)	17 yrs (YPU)	18 yrs (OW)	18 yrs (YPU)
April	3	11	6	9	8	14	21	5
May	2	14	4	8	13	10	14	3
June	7	22	1	11	7	10	16	2
July	Nil	34	10	11	9	7	14	3
August	4	19	1	10	9	11	19	8
September	3	23	4	22	9	14	14	5
October	3	19	8	13	8	10	16	4
November	1	22	4	14	9	14	13	4
December	Nil	15	3	12	7	5	13	2
January	2	23	Nil	11	10	10	8	4
February	2	19	8	13	16	7	16	5
March	1	30	4	15	10	5	18	4
Totals	28	251	53	149	115	117	182	49

Table 2. Monthly totals of admissions on young persons unit (YPU) and totals of young persons admitted to other wards (OW), April 1994 to March 1995

Month	15 yrs (OW)	15 yrs (YPU)	16 yrs (OW)	16 yrs (YPU)	17 yrs (OW)	17 yrs (YPU)	18 yrs (OW)	18 yrs (YPU)
April	Nil	23	Nil	21	7	15	10	4
May	Nil	21	Nil	15	9	13	15	3
June	Nil	25	4	16	8	9	14	4
July	Nil	25	3	27	5	8	13	1
August	Nil	30	Nil	17	10	13	11	7
September	Nil	21	1	21	10	7	23	2
October	Nil	35	Nil	24	2	16	8	2
November	Nil	14	1	21	2	20	18	4
December	1	14	3	11	7	2	16	2
January	Nil	24	1	19	5	11	17	4
February	Nil	13	3	13	7	13	12	7
March	1	41	1	15	4	17	10	7
Totals	2	286	17	217	76	144	167	47

length of stay is 2.7 days with an overall bed occupancy of between 76.3% and 86.2%. These figures acknowledge that other professionals are becoming aware of the needs of children and teenagers. The total number of consultants using the ward has now increased to 44. The monitoring of standards and the evaluation of patient satisfaction surveys has shown that the ward provides a high level of care which meets the patients' needs and often exceeds their expectations. It is therefore an extremely popular facility and more often than not the demand for it outstrips the availability of beds.

Improving the service

As the ward has become established the nursing staff have begun to develop a greater insight into the needs of adolescents. Recent project work includes the development of a nursing model for adolescents/teenagers which is proving to be very specific to this client group's needs. During its development thoughts and opinions were obtained from the teenagers. It is very much directed towards self-care, which supports the World Health Organisation concept[6] that the involvement of young people in their own health care is more inclined to lead to a successful outcome.

A randomised monthly patient satisfaction survey (Fig 3) has, however, shown a loophole in the service. We found that only 15%

CHECKLIST FOR USERS – EMERALD WARD

DATE OF AUDIT   SPECIALTY

PLEASE COMPLETE BY TICKING EITHER 'YES' OR 'NO'

1. Are you:
    male?   female?

2. How old are you?

3. Did the doctors ask you if you would prefer to be admitted to: **Yes   No**
    A. children's ward?
    B. adolescent area?
    C. adult ward?

4. Did the nurse involve you in the planning of your care?

5. Do you think the way the ward has been decorated makes it:
    A. colourful?
    B. gloomy?

6. Do you consider that privacy is satisfactory in:
    A. sleeping areas?
    B. washroom and showers?
    C. recreational areas?

7. Have you found the staff friendly and approachable?
    A. the doctors
    B. the nurses
    C. other staff

8. Do you feel that you can talk to staff in confidence about personal matters?

9. Were you able to keep in contact with your friends and family by:
    A. using the phone?
    B. visiting?

10. Do you find that the food is:
    A. good?
    B. average?
    C. horrible?
    Was there enough choice?
    Was the food hot enough?

11. Were the amusement activities available suited to your age group?

12. Can you suggest any other games or pastimes that you
    would like available?

13. During your stay in hospital, is there anything you would like to change?

Fig 3. *Checklist for monthly patient satisfaction survey*

Charter for

Adolescent Patients

Statement

Adolescence is a time of major physical, psychological and social change. Therefore, the needs of the Adolescent are different from the needs of both the child and the adult.

All Adolescent Patients:

1. Aged 11 to 16 years will be nursed in the place appropriate to their needs. Emerald Ward (D7 West) Royal Gwent Hospital.

2. Aged 16 to 19 years will be made aware of the special facilities available on Emerald Ward and be allowed to make an informed decision as to where they wish to be nursed.

3. Have the right to be informed about their medical condition and care. They will be allowed to participate in decisions concerning their treatment.

4. Will be able to discuss their physical and emotional problems in confidence with appropriately trained staff who understand their needs and respect their growing need for independence.

5. Need privacy and must at all times be treated with honesty, tact and sensitivity.

6. Who are chronically sick or disabled should have appropriate care which takes this into account.

7. Will have care which is sympathetic to their Ethnic and Cultural needs.

8. Will have the opportunity to maintain contact with family and friends. Parents should be allowed to visit freely and have facilities provided for overnight stay if they request them.

9. Will be provided with space for recreational activities and a quiet room provided for study when needed.

10. Who cannot be nursed on Emerald Ward need staff who will seek advice about their care from the specialised staff of Emerald Ward to ensure their emotional and psychological needs are met.

© Glan Hafren NHS Trust

Fig 4. *Charter for adolescent patients*

of teenagers aged between 16 and 19 years were being offered the choice of where they wished to be cared for. It was therefore decided that a Charter for Adolescent Patients should be developed,

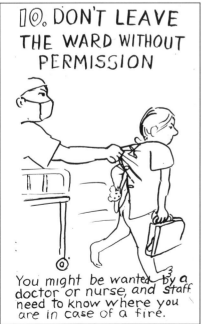

Fig 5. *Examples of how the 'house rules' are displayed in the young persons unit*

and this has now been fully approved by the Trust and has been circulated throughout the organisation (Fig 4). Following the implementation of the charter we hope to see a decrease of 17 to 18 year olds on the adult wards. Other projects are regular reviews of the ward philosophy, the introduction and evaluation of self-medication, which is under trial with our cystic fibrosis patients. More recently we have tried to create a more relaxed atmosphere by introducing the wearing of street clothing for nursing staff.

Regular 'in house' lectures are also arranged for staff which relate specifically to teenager problems. It is not only the staff who are responsible for establishing the ward philosophy, but our patients are also asked for comments on how we can improve the service, and from this ten house rules have been developed and agreed. The rules are displayed on a board within the ward; each has a character relating to the specific rule with a brief rationale underneath (Fig 5). The teenagers are shown the house rules as part of their orientation to the ward. We feel the house rules have enhanced the respect and understanding between staff and patients, allowing a relaxed atmosphere but also a sense of discipline.

Conclusion

This is a brief overview of what we have managed to establish within the hospital for adolescent inpatients. A further achievement has been the establishment of an evening diabetic clinic for adolescents, which is held on a fortnightly basis and which has a 90% uptake.

We hope to develop the services that adolescents require even further so as to include an asthma clinic for adolescents.

The explosive and challenging nature of the adolescent age group can make many demands on nursing and medical staff which often require much individual attention. This can be difficult for other health professionals to understand, and it is therefore up to health professionals who regularly work with young people to promote and educate other colleagues.

Our adolescents are happy. Are yours?

References

1. *The Welfare of Children in Hospital.* Report of the Committee of Central Health Services Council (Chairman: Sir Harry Platt). London: HMSO, 1959.
2. *Fit for the Future.* Report of the Committee on Child Health Services (Chairman: Prof. S.D.M. Court). London: HMSO, 1976.

3. *Caring for Children in the Health Service. Where are the children?* London: CCHS, 1987. (Available from NAWCH.)
4. National Association for the Welfare of Children in Hospital. Quality Review. *Setting Standards for Adolescents in Hospital.* London: NAWCH, 1990.
5. World Health Organisation. *The Health of Youth* (Background Document). Geneva: WHO, 1989.
6. British Paediatric Association. *The Needs and Care of Adolescents* (Report of a BPA Working Party). St Andrews Place, London: BPA, 1986.
7. Rodin J. *Are your adolescents happy? Standards of Care.* THS. September 1990.
8. Thornes R. *Parents Staying Overnight with Their Children.* London: Caring for Children in the Health Service, 1986.

PART THREE

Specific
medical problems

7 | Injuries to adolescents

Jo Sibert
Professor of Community Child Health,
University of Wales College of Medicine

As we increasingly focus on health of adolescents, we realise the importance of injuries as a cause of death, disability and use of NHS resources in teenagers. Injuries are the most common cause of death in those aged between 15 and 18 years:[1] in England and Wales in 1992 injuries accounted for 64% of deaths in young men and 44% of deaths in young women. Injuries also cause many young people to be disabled and a fifth of the adolescent population present to the Accident and Emergency Department in a year. These injuries present formidable problems both in surveillance and in prevention.

Deaths to adolescents from injuries

Injury is overwhelmingly the most common cause of death in young men. This may be as a result of an accident or may be non-accidental (Table 1).

Table 1. Deaths, England and Wales, 15–19 years, 1992

	Male	Female	Total
All deaths	969	432	1,401
Deaths from injury			
Accidental	460	142	602
Non-accidental	100	32	132
Undetermined	59	18	77
Total from injuries	619	192	811

Source: OPCS

A closer analysis of these deaths shows that the vast majority are due to transport injuries (Table 2). This toll of young people killed on the roads either in cars or as pedestrians must be of major concern to society.

Table 2. Deaths from accidental injuries and poisoning, England and Wales, 15–19 years, 1992

Cause	Male	Female	Total
Transport accidents	376	110	486
Accidental poisoning	24	14	38
Accidental falls	13	6	19
Fire and flames	1	5	6
Accidental drowning	24	2	26
Inhalation	13	2	15
Others	9	3	12
Total	460	142	602

Disability following injury in the adolescent

We know relatively little about the prevalence of disability from injuries to adolescents. Barker and Power[2] estimated from work from the National Child Development Study that the prevalence of permanent disability at the age of 23 following an injury was 28 per 1,000. The prevalence of registered disability in the same sample was 10 per 1,000. These are both significant figures. Rivara and his colleagues in the United States found that up to 55.1% of young people had limitations in their activities during the week following an injury.[3]

Less serious injuries to adolescents

As well as causing death and disability injuries also cause less serious problems to adolescents. Presentations to the Accident and Emergency Department at the Cardiff Royal Infirmary in 14–18 year olds for 1992 are shown in Table 3.[4] (I am grateful to Dr Rupert Evans for these figures.) In the year the total number of cases presenting was 5,410. This represented over one in five of the population in the City of Cardiff. Work from the National Child Development Study[2] confirms this high prevalence of injury with

Table 3. Accident and emergency presentations, 14–18 years: Cardiff Royal Infirmary, 1993

Type of injury	%	Place of injury	%
Accident	53.6	Home	29.9
Sport	17.6	Public place	26.5
Assault	6.8	Sport	18.1
Medical	6.3	Education	13
Self injury	2.2	Work	4
Others	13.5	Road traffic accidents	3.4
		Others	5.1

62% of men and 26% of women reporting injuries requiring hospital treatment between the ages of 16 and 23 years.

Accidents remain the largest cause of these presentations at 55%. However, significant numbers of young people are injured by sport and by assaults. We know that alcohol[5] and experience with previous violent abhorrent behaviour[6] are associated with assaults and accidental injuries in this age group. Assaults are therefore not random events but an association with a particular lifestyle, particularly in young men.

Transport injuries

In childhood pedestrian road traffic accidents are the most common cause of transport injury. In contrast in adolescence, deaths in cars outnumber other causes. Table 4 shows the numbers of young people killed in transport accidents in England and Wales in 1992.[1] Over 300 young people were killed in cars. Although alcohol clearly plays some part in these deaths, the phenomenon of 'joy riding' and taking away cars has been part of this problem, which remains a major challenge.

Some young people die from motor cycle accidents and the rate of road accident deaths and serious injuries reaches a peak at 19 years. Young people also injure themselves on bicycles. We know that wearing cycle helmets will prevent some of the serious effects of head injuries from bicycle injuries.[7] However, campaigns aimed at young people have not on the whole been successful. Joshi, Beckett and Macfarlane in 1994 state we should not be too optimistic, however, about the extent that health education can increase helmet use.[8] Even very imaginative health education may not overcome the compelling counter-pressures operating in this area.

Table 4. The numbers of young people killed in transport accidents in England and Wales in 1992

	Male	Female	Total
Transport accidents			
Railway	6	0	6
Motor vehicle	367	108	475
Other	3	2	5
Total	376	110	486
Motor vehicle accidents			
Cycles	21	4	25
Pedestrian	37	21	58
In cars	232	72	304
Motor cycles	73	11	84
Non traffic	4	0	4
Total	367	108	475

Drowning

Drowning is also an important cause of death in young people. We analysed deaths in children under 14 in England and Wales in 1988 and 1989.[9] We found that playing about in rivers, canals, lakes and the sea by older children was an important cause of death, with 56 children drowning in rivers, canals and lakes and 20 in the sea. There is no reason to suspect that patterns are different in young people. Swimming ability in municipal swimming pools may not be related to swimming ability in lakes and the sea. There is evidence from Australia and other parts of the world that life-guarding of beaches and other swimming areas is helpful in preventing drowning.[10]

Sports injuries

Participating in sport is a major part of recreation for young people. We do know that young people frequently present with sport injuries and some die. Specific types of recreational activity cause particular problems, eg neck injuries tend to occur in rugby football,[11] and head and back injuries in horse riding accidents. Epidemiological studies followed by work with the game authorities seems the best way forward in dealing with this kind of problem.

Injuries to young people at work and at school

Young people spend time at school, where they may be at risk from sports injuries. Increasingly, however, they also belong to the world of work. This may be part time or part of a planned transition to working life. Evidence on injuries in work for young people is difficult to find. There is some anecdotal evidence that they may be at increased risk. Young people in farms are at special risk because they may live and work in the same place.[12]

Violence and non-accidental injury

Non-accidental deaths in young people are also a problem. In 1992 132 young people died from non-accidental injury (Table 5). Of these, 22 were homicide and 110 were suicide. The death rates in young men from suicide have caused particular concern with a doubling in the rates from 1975 to 1990. We have recently analysed hanging in young people[13] and this remains a particular cause of suicide that gives rise to much concern.

Table 5. Non-accidental deaths in young people in England and Wales, 1992

Non-accidental deaths	Male	Female	Total
Suicide and self inflicted	87	23	110
Homicide	13	9	22
Total	100	32	132

In the United States firearm injuries to young people are one of the major causes of death and disability. Rates in the UK are much lower, but there is some evidence that these deaths and disability are increasing and we, as a society, need to take much more care about the development of firearms, particularly in the drug culture in some inner city areas.

We must also remember that non-accidental injury particularly associated with sexual abuse continues to be a problem in young people. Young people under the age of 18 are still subject to the Children Act and are appropriately dealt with under the Child Protection procedures.

Solutions for preventing injuries in adolescents

Solutions to the prevention of accidents to young people are not easy. There is very little evidence that education influences the behaviour of young people significantly and it has been changing the environment that has prevented accidents to children.[14] For instance there are at least five case control studies that show the effectiveness of cycle helmets in preventing head injury.[15-19] Thompson *et al*[14] in Seattle studied 235 patients with head injuries, using as controls two groups of patients with bicycle injuries not involving the head. Only 7% of the case patients had been wearing helmets, compared with 24% of emergency room controls and 23% of the second control group. Of 99 cyclists with serious head injury only 4% wore helmets. Cyclists had an 85% reduction in their risk of head injury when wearing helmets.

There are many other examples where environmental change has prevented injuries, from flame-proofing children's night wear,[20] through child-resistant containers preventing poisoning,[21] to traffic calming.[22] This needs to be remembered in planning injury strategies for children or young people. Until recently most research and clinical effort has been confined to preventing injuries in children under 14. Although there are many sad problems associated with injuries to children, injury rates in young people are also very high, particularly from transport accidents and particularly to young people in cars. This is a subject that needs further analysis and research.

References

1. Office of Population Censuses and Surveys. *Mortality statistics.* London: OPCS, 1992.
2. Barker M, Power C. Disability in young adults: the role of injuries. *Journal of Epidemiology and Community Health* 1993; **47**(5): 349–54.
3. Rivara FP, Thompson RS, Thompson DC, Calonge N. Injuries to children and adolescents: impact on physical health. *Pediatrics* 1991; **88**: 783–8.
4. Evans R. Personal communication, 1995.
5. Shepherd JP, Farrington DP. Assault as a public health problem: discussion paper. *Journal of the Royal Society of Medicine* 1993; **86**(2): 89–92.
6. Rivara FP, Shepherd JP, Farrington DP, Richmond PW, Cannon P. The victim as offender in youth violence. Personal communication.
7. Thompson RS, Rivara FP, Thompson DC. A case-control study of the effectiveness of bicycle safety helmets. *New England Journal of Medicine* 1989; **320**: 1361–7.
8. Joshi MS, Beckett K, Macfarlane A. *Archives of Disease in Childhood* 1994; **71**: 536–9.

9. Kemp AM, Sibert JR. Drowning and near drowning in children in the United Kingdom: lessons for prevention. *British Medical Journal* 1992; **304**: 1143–6.

10. Nixon J, Pearn J, Wilkey I, Corcoran A. A fifteen year study of child drowning. *Accident Analysis and Prevention* 1986; **18**: 199–203.

11. Noakes T, Jakoet I. Spinal cord injuries in rugby union players. *British Medical Journal* 1995; **310**: 1345–6.

12. Cameron D, Bishop C, Sibert JR. Farm accidents in children. *British Medical Journal* 1992; **305**: 23–5.

13. Nixon JW, Kemp AM, Levene S, Sibert JR. Suffocation, choking and strangulation in childhood in England and Wales: epidemiology and prevention. *Archives of Disease in Childhood* 1995; **72**: 6–11.

14. Sibert JR. Accidents to children: the doctor's role—education or environmental change. *Archives of Disease in Childhood* 1991; **66**: 890–4.

15. Thompson R, Rivara FP, Thompson DCA. Case control study on the effectiveness of bicycle safety helmets. *New England Journal of Medicine* 1989; **320**: 1361–7.

16. Malmaris C, Summers CL, Browning C, Palmer CR. Injury patterns in cyclists attending an accident and emergency department: a comparison of helmet wearers and non-wearers. *British Medical Journal* 1994; **308**: 1537–40.

17. Thomas S, Acton C, Nixon J, Battistutta D, Pitt WR, Clark R. Effectiveness of bicycle helmets in preventing injury in children: a case control study. *British Medical Journal* 1994; **308**: 173–6.

18. McDermott FT, Lane JC, Brazenor GA, Debney EA. The effectiveness of bicycle helmets: a study of 1,710 casualties. *Journal of Trauma* 1993; **34**: 834–44.

19. Spaite DW, Murphy M, Criss EA, Valenzuela TD, Meislin HW. A prospective analysis of injury severity among helmeted and non-helmeted bicyclists involved in collisions with motor vehicles. *Journal of Trauma* 1991; **31**: 1510–6.

20. Carr MJT. Trends in causes of fatal burns in children. *Lancet* 1978; **i**: 1199.

21. Sibert JR, Craft AW, Jackson RH. Child resistant packaging and accidental child poisoning. *Lancet* 1977; **ii**: 289–90.

22. Royal Dutch Touring Club (1977). Woonerf Club, PO Box 93200, The Hague, The Netherlands.

8 | Growth and puberty

Elizabeth C Crowne
Clinical Lecturer in Paediatric Endocrinology,
John Radcliffe Hospital, Oxford

David B Dunger
Consultant Paediatric Endocrinologist,
John Radcliffe Hospital, Oxford

Normal pubertal growth and development

Puberty is the process of acquiring reproductive function and is recognised by the appearance of secondary sexual characteristics and an associated spurt in growth. The sequence of events of physical changes during this period of development is essentially constant with a tight relationship between the timing of the growth spurt and the stage of pubertal development (Fig 1). The loss or interruption of this consonance of puberty indicates abnormal pubertal development and requires investigation.

In the majority of boys, the first clinical change of puberty is testicular enlargement. The average age at the first appearance of testicular volumes of 4 ml is 12.0 years and has occurred in 95% of British boys by the age 14.0 years.[1] The first clinical change in female puberty is the appearance of a breastbud, mean age 11.5 years and this has occurred in 95% of girls by 13.2 years. Pubic and axillary hair growth is a manifestation of adrenal androgen secretion. Breast and pubic hair development usually proceed in parallel. Menarche usually occurs at breast stage 4 and pubic hair stage 4.

Boys enter puberty approximately 6 months later than girls, and have their growth spurt at a later stage of puberty. Prepubertal height velocity shows a gradual decline until it reaches a nadir, just prior to the growth spurt. The growth spurt in boys is associated with 10–12 ml testicular volume and in girls with breast stage 2 or 3. Mean (SD) peak height velocity is 8.8 (1.05) cm/year and 8.13 (0.78) cm/year for boys and girls respectively.[2] The longer period of growth before peak height velocity and brisker growth spurt in boys accounts for the 12.5 cm difference in adult height between the

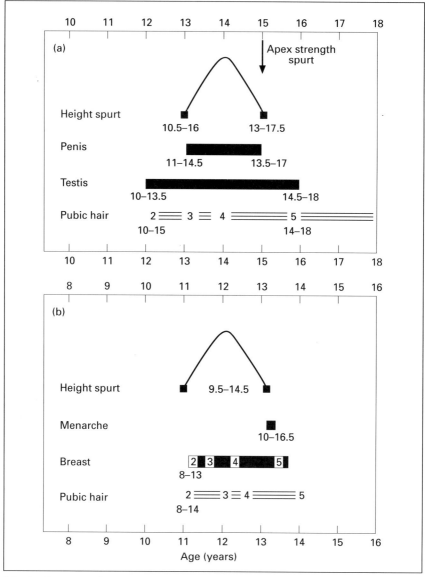

Fig 1. *Sequence of events in normal puberty for (a) boys and (b) girls.*[67] Reproduced with permission from: Tanner JM. *Growth at adolescence.* 2nd edn. Oxford: Blackwell Scientific Publications, 1962.

sexes (Fig 2). Puberty is completed in 2–3 years in 50% of normal boys and girls, and in 5 years in 97%.

Variations in the timing of puberty

Many factors affect growth and the tempo of maturation. There

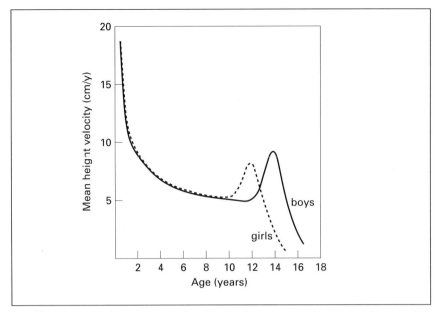

Fig 2. *Mean height velocity in boys and girls showing the earlier but smaller growth spurt of girls*

are complex interactions between genetic and environmental factors in which the level of nutrition and incidence of disease play pivotal roles. These factors account for many differences between Western and Third World patterns of growth and development.[3] To ensure a valid assessment of an individual's growth pattern, it is essential to have standards relevant to that individual's population.[1] Even so the pattern of growth and development of populations is not static, but subject to secular trends, with a general trend for taller stature and earlier maturation. This trend is strongly associated with indices of improving economic wellbeing in populations and is reflected in the new UK charts.[4]

There are well-recognised associations within a population between fatness, growth and the timing of puberty.[5] Fat children tend to be taller and enter puberty at an earlier age. Buckler (1990) in his longitudinal study of Leeds children found that the fatter children were taller prepubertally, but that this difference did not persist during puberty and did not result in a taller final adult height.[6] In the girls there was a correlation between fatness and an earlier puberty but this was not evident in the boys. In a longitudinal study of 78 boys in the USA,[7] the timing of puberty was significantly correlated with body size in the first year of life and did not correlate with indices of nutrition, in a well-nourished, non-obese population of boys. Final adult height is not adversely affected by the timing of puberty,[8] except in precocious puberty, although the percentage of height achieved during the pubertal growth spurt will be affected. Peak height velocity is negatively correlated with age and so the earlier puberty is begun the greater the peak height velocity attained; those who enter puberty later have a smaller growth spurt but they will have achieved a greater height from their prepubertal growth.[9]

The events that initiate normal puberty are not clearly understood. The changes of puberty require the synergistic action of growth hormone (GH) and sex steroids and therefore intact hypothalamic–pituitary–gonadal and hypothalamic–pituitary–insulin-like growth factor (IGF-1) axes, the permissive action of thyroid hormones and interactions with insulin and nutrition. Subsequent reproductive and sexual function are controlled by the hypothalamic–pituitary–gonadal axis.

Endocrine regulation of puberty

The hypothalamic–pituitary–gonadal axis has been shown to be active in the first 2 years of life and levels of gonadotrophins and sex steroids may be as high as those observed in puberty.[10] Serum gonadotrophin and testosterone levels then fall to low basal levels by 3–6 months. Studies using highly sensitive gonadotrophin assays have identified low pulsatile secretion of luteinising hormone (LH), and therefore, by inference also gonadotrophin-releasing hormone (GnRH) secretion, with a definite circadian rhythm in prepubertal children.[11,12] Nevertheless the activity of the axis is much reduced with low or undetectable serum LH and testosterone levels and a much reduced testosterone and LH response to administration of human chorionic gonadotrophin (HCG) or GnRH respectively. The mechanism of hypothalamic—pituitary suppression in the prepubertal period is not clear.

The onset of puberty is characterised by sleep-associated increase in pulsatile LH secretion, which can be detected before clinical signs of puberty.[12] This increase in LH pulsatility could reflect changes in endogenous GnRH secretion, changes in the sensitivity of the pituitary to GnRH and/or alteration in the threshold of response to the negative feedback of gonadal steroids at the hypothalamus or pituitary. Increases in both frequency and amplitude of LH pulses in puberty have been reported by some,[13,14] although others report only an increase in LH frequency.[11] Wu *et al* (1989) propose augmentation of sleep-associated GnRH pulsatility as the key event at the onset of puberty.[15] This primes the pituitary to amplify the GnRH signal, initially just at night, but as pituitary responsiveness increases further in midpuberty, the small amplitude GnRH pulses are also transmitted during the day. There is also evidence indicating qualitative as well as quantitative changes in LH with increasing bioactivity of LH at each pubertal stage as puberty progresses,[16,17] and increased pituitary reserve of bioactive LH in boys at midpuberty.[18] A recent larger cross-sectional study of changes in bioactive and immunoactive LH in overnight profiles in normal pubertal children found an increase in the ratio of LH bio:immuno-activity with the onset of nocturnal pulsatility in early puberty, concordance between bio- and immuno-active LH pulsatility and a close association with sex steroids as a testosterone rise always followed an LH pulse.[19]

In boys testosterone levels start to rise in response to increasing LH pulsatility, initially just at night, and eventually throughout the day (Fig 3). Sex hormone-binding globulin (SHBG) levels fall in both normal male and female puberty.[20] This fall combined with the rise in testosterone secretion further increases the availability of bioactive testosterone. Rising nocturnal testosterone then begins to exert negative feedback and initiates a deceleration in nocturnal GnRH/LH frequency into the adult range.[21]

In girls positive feedback by sex steroids develops at midpuberty.[22] The ovary, which is a small structure with a few follicles prepubertally, develops a multicystic morphology once nocturnal gonadotrophic secretion is established. Oestrogen is secreted by

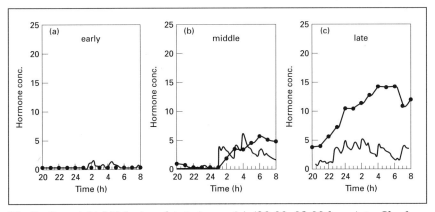

Fig 3. *Overnight LH (—) and testosterone (•) (20.00–08.00 hours) profiles from a boy in (a) early, (b) middle and (c) late puberty. In early puberty there are nocturnal pulses of LH only with undetectable testosterone levels. Increasing LH pulsatility then results in a rising nocturnal testosterone level. Later LH pulses and testosterone are also detectable during the day*

ovarian follicle cells, and circulates bound to SHBG to reach target tissues in the breast, uterus, adipocyte and bone. Positive feedback at the pituitary from a rising oestrogen level then triggers an LH surge which stimulates ovulation from a dominant follicle. A dominant follicle can develop once there is 24 hour gonadotrophin secretion. A cycle may be established by midpuberty. The uterus changes from a prepubertal tubular structure to a pear-shaped structure with increasing oestradiol secretion from the ovary and there is an increase in depth of the endometrium just before menarche. In the first two years following menarche 55–90% of cycles may be anovulatory, but by 5 years only 20% are still anovulatory.

An increase in GH secretion coincident with the pubertal growth spurt occurs in males and females, and is an amplitude modulated process.[23-25] Studies in children who are GH and gonadotrophin deficient have indicated that both GH and androgens are required to produce an adequate pubertal growth spurt.[26,27] Sex steroids appear to augment stimulated GH levels when administered pharmacologically,[28] and during spontaneous puberty.[29] Pharmacologically induced puberty also results in an increase in GH levels,[30,31] and conversely the suppression of precocious puberty with long-acting GnRH analogue results in a decrease in GH levels.[32,33] Correlations between testosterone levels and circulating GH pulse characteristics have been reported in growing boys,[24] although not in postpubertal or young adult subjects when GH secretion has decreased but testosterone levels remain elevated. Others report a correlation between oestradiol levels and GH in adults.[34] Oestrogen 'priming' has been shown to result in increased growth in pre- and early pubertal boys[35] and increased peak GH responses to pharmacological tests.[36] These data would suggest that it is aromatisation of testosterone to oestradiol, and not testosterone itself, that is necessary for the augmentation of GH secretion in puberty. In addition androgen blockade with flutamide in late pubertal males resulted in an increase in GH secretion, possibly as a result of increased stimulation of oestrogen receptor-mediated pathways.[37] Androgen-resistant individuals (with testicular feminisation) were reported to have a pubertal growth spurt resembling a female growth spurt (mean age 12.4 years, peak height velocity 7.4 cm/year), suggesting that oestrogen alone without androgens can stimulate pubertal growth.[38] The sensitivity of the regulation of GH secretion to very low levels of oestradiol is suggested by the observation that an increase in GH secretion in girls may precede any clinical sign of puberty.[25]

Sex steroids are therefore essential for a normal pubertal growth spurt through their action on endogenous GH secretion. They also determine the limit of adult height by their action on skeletal maturation and closure of the epiphyseal plate. Thus in untreated hypogonadotrophic hypogonadism there is pubertal delay but normal, or even an increase in, final adult height as the epiphyses do not close and growth can continue for longer.[39] Precocious puberty, however, compromises final adult height because although there is a growth spurt there is also rapid skeletal maturation and early closure of the epiphyses.

The increase in GH at puberty is associated with an increase in IGF-1, and insulin levels which increase progressively during puberty and then decline to prepubertal levels in adults.[40] The pubertal rise in insulin compensates for the well-recognised increase in insulin resistance found at puberty which is specifically a defect in peripheral glucose metabolism and allows amplification of the anabolic effects of insulin on protein metabolism.[41] Holly (1989) in a cross-sectional study reported a decrease in IGF binding protein-1 (IGFBP-1) levels throughout childhood as fasting levels of insulin rose.[42] IGFBP-1 is inversely regulated by insulin and as IGFBP-1 appears to be an inhibitor of IGF bioactivity,[43] the normal pubertal fall may be one mechanism whereby nutrition regulates the rate of pubertal maturation. Thus, the raised insulin levels, acting via modification of SHBG and IGFBPs, are a means of integrating growth, pubertal development and nutritional status in puberty.

Early puberty

Appearance of secondary sexual characteristics before the age of 8 years in a girl and 9 years in a boy requires investigation. It is essential to establish at the outset whether there is consonance of secondary sexual characteristics, growth and bone maturity indicating the onset of true (or centrally driven) puberty. Of particular concern are boys presenting with early puberty, who are more likely to have a pathological cause, whereas although girls present far more frequently, they are more likely to have an idiopathic central precocious puberty. Children presenting with signs and symptoms not consistent with a normal puberty must be investigated at any age. For instance, in a boy penile enlargement and pubic hair development without testicular enlargement, or in a girl clitoromegaly, pubic and axillary hair indicate excess androgens either from the adrenal (eg congenital adrenal hyperplasia (CAH) or tumour) or a virilising tumour of the ovary or dysgenetic gonad. Oestrogen secreting tumours can also occur, eg in the ovary, and present with signs of oestrogenisation alone such as breast development or vaginal bleeding.

Early breast development

Premature thelarche

Early breast development with no other clinical signs of puberty, changes in growth velocity or advance in bone age is not an uncommon presentation in the first 2 years of life. In the immediate neonatal period this is due to exposure to maternal oestrogens and soon disappears. Nevertheless it may persist or recur. Pelvic ultrasound examination may then identify an isolated ovarian cyst, but an immature uterus. In addition follicle-stimulating hormone (FSH) levels may be raised. This is a benign, self-limiting condition which requires no further investigation other than clinical examination, growth assessment and pelvic ultrasound.

Thelarche variant

In this condition girls present with early breast development and some other signs of puberty, eg some increase in growth rate and advanced bone age but an immature uterus and ovary on ultrasound examination. It has been proposed that this may be due to isolated pulsatile FSH secretion and have a good prognosis for growth.[44] No active treatment is indicated unless breast development itself causes problems, although growth and pubertal development should be followed carefully.

Precocious puberty

A child with precocious puberty presents with the normal signs and symptoms of puberty but at an early age (girls <8 years, boys <9 years). Thus girls have breast enlargement, pubic hair and an increased growth velocity; boys testicular enlargement, genital development, pubic hair and an increased growth velocity. Precocious puberty can be either gonadotrophin dependent or gonadotrophin independent. The former is more common, and is secondary to premature activation of the GnRH pulse generator either because of the early onset of normal puberty or secondary to intracranial pathology. The latter rare condition occurs when there is autonomous secretion of sex steroids from the gonads, ie gonadotrophin levels are low. Assessment of a child presenting with precocious puberty requires growth measurement, pubertal staging, clinical examination with particular attention to neurological examination, visual field assessment and fundoscopy and a bone age estimation. In the female, where there are no other unusual signs or symptoms and pelvic ultrasound may show multicystic ovaries with an enlarging uterus, no further investigations are required in those over the age of 8. Imaging of the brain is mandatory, preferably an MRI, if there are any neurological signs or symptoms, and in all boys irrespective of age. Intracranial causes of precocious puberty include hydrocephalus, congenital malformations such as hypothalamic hamartomas, trauma, cranial irradiation and tumours such as pineal tumours, germinomas and optic gliomas (eg in neurofibromatosis). Rarely gonadotrophin secreting tumours may occur. Intracranial teratomas or germ cell tumours and hepatoblastomas can produce HCG, and pituitary adenomas secreting gonadotrophins have also been described.

Management obviously requires treatment of any underlying cause, such as an intracranial tumour. This will not necessarily alter the progression of precocious puberty, and management of this problem requires careful assessment of the physical, psychological and emotional effects of early development. In older children, there may not be significant problems and active intervention is not indicated (Fig 4). If there are significant psychological problems, and where there are concerns about growth and advanced bone age, the progress of puberty can be stopped with GnRH analogues.[45] Because of their sustained action, these analogues downregulate the pulsatile gonadotrophin signal and hence stop sex steroid secretion. They can be given intranasally, subcutaneously or by depot injection. Monthly injections of the depot preparation are probably the most effective in terms of suppressing secondary sexual characteristics, although there is increasing evidence that lost height potential associated with rapid skeletal maturation is not recovered.[46] Studies are underway investigating whether the administration of GH with GnRH analogues may improve final height prognosis.[47]

Gonadotrophin independent puberty

This rare condition presents with the signs of precocious puberty except investigation reveals raised sex steroid levels in the absence of gonadotrophin pulsatility as the gonads are active independently. There may be discordant signs of puberty, eg girls presenting with menstruation with only early breast development, associated with

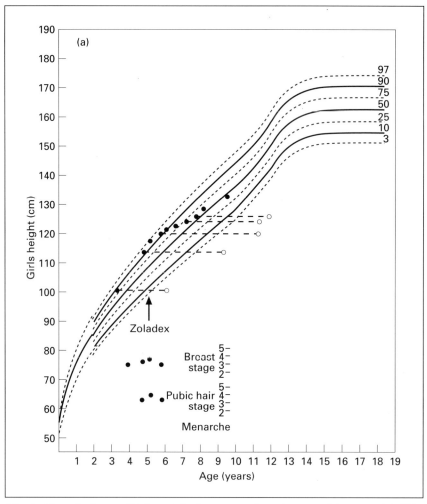

Fig 4. *Growth charts of (a) a girl who presented at the age of 4 years with idio-pathic central precocious puberty. She has been treated with a luteinising-hormone-releasing hormone (GnRH) analogue with resolution of her secondary sexual char-acteristics and slowing of her growth velocity but no improvement in her advanced bone age; (b) a boy who presented at 6.6 years with precocious puberty caused by a hypothalamic hamartoma who did not have any treatment to stop his pubertal development. After an early pubertal growth spurt he ended up with a significantly reduced adult height compared with his mid-parental height*

skin pigmentation and bony abnormalities as part of the McCune–Albright syndrome, a condition in which there is continuous activation of the intracellular messenger of gonadotrophin action due to abnormalities of the G protein.[48] Testotoxicosis is an inherited gonadotrophin independent puberty recently shown to be

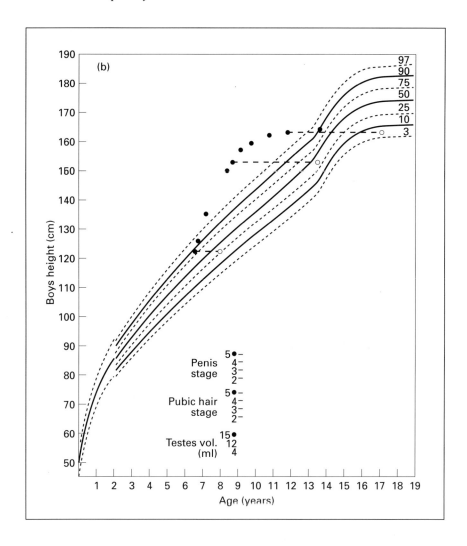

caused by a mutation of the LH receptor gene, resulting in constant activation without LH binding.[49] Treatment of both conditions involves suppression of the effects of sex steroids at tissue level with anti-oestrogens or anti-androgens.

Late puberty

The diagnosis of delayed puberty is generally made when there is no evidence of sexual maturation at an age when 97% of a normal population will have entered puberty, that is a boy who does not have testicular volume of 4 ml by the age of 14 years or a girl who has no evidence of breast budding by 13.2 years. One would have anticipated that constitutional delay of growth and puberty

(CDGP) should occur with equal frequency in both sexes. However typically it is a boy who presents, often with a family history of delayed maturation. There are several possible explanations for this sex difference. It may be a consequence of the fact that the growth spurt begins at an earlier stage of puberty in girls. Alternatively there may be much greater concern amongst parents about the potential short stature of a son rather than a daughter. Others believe that the sex difference reflects the fact that girls secrete gonadotrophins from the pituitary at a lower threshold of GnRH stimulation than boys.[31] Correct diagnosis and appropriate management requires an understanding of events surrounding the onset of puberty and the normal sequence of events in puberty.

Typically there has been a pattern of delayed growth throughout childhood with growth velocities at the lower limit of normal and heights at the lower end of the target height range. Nevertheless the children and their parents become particularly concerned at the time of normal puberty when the delay in onset of puberty and the growth spurt makes the deviation from normal more marked. The differential diagnosis of CDGP will cover a wide range of paediatric diseases. In the history there may be features suggestive of asthma, coeliac disease or other chronic systemic disorders which may be associated with poor growth and delayed puberty. The examination should include a general assessment and, in particular, search for signs of Turner's syndrome, hypothyroidism, visual field defects, fundal abnormalities and skeletal disproportion. Assessment of pubertal status and accurate height measurement are essential, with the estimation of growth velocity over a minimum period of 3 months. A low threshold for investigating such a child should be maintained, however. The presence of symptoms such as recurrent headache, a borderline growth velocity or an incongruity in the pattern of pubertal development should arouse suspicion leading to biochemical and/or radiological investigations, and in girls a karyotype to exclude Turner's syndrome. Nevertheless, the history, physical examination and a knowledge of the growth velocity will allow the diagnosis to be made in the majority of cases without recourse to biochemical investigations, and the bone age estimation will provide an indication of the remaining time for growth and permit height prediction.

It is well recognised that children with CDGP may appear to be biochemically GH insufficient in the late prepubertal years until the onset of the growth spurt.[50] Therefore if tests of GH secretion are deemed necessary to distinguish CDGP from isolated GH deficiency then 'priming' with sex steroids is indicated.[36] Basal gonadotrophins should be measured to exclude gonadal failure but the most difficult differential diagnosis lies in the distinction between CDGP and isolated hypogonadotrophic hypogonadism as in both conditions basal gonadotrophins are low and gonadotrophin response to GnRH stimulation may be prepubertal. Numerous tests have been devised to try and distinguish between the two diagnoses but none does so reliably and as in clinical practice most of the children presenting with delayed puberty have CDGP such tests are rather futile. It is not reasonable to delay induction of puberty and the appropriate time to insist upon a definite diagnosis is after the completion of 'induced' puberty. At this stage the differential diagnosis is usually very easy and, in most instances, can be confirmed by estimating the basal FSH, LH and testosterone (oestradiol) levels off sex steroid replacement.

There are several studies following boys with untreated CDGP through to final height, demonstrating that as a group they reach their predicted adult height, although not all studies indicate that they reach their genetic target as represented by their mid-parental height.[51-53] The discrepancies between these reports may simply reflect a selection bias in that those boys with CDGP who are particularly short in the context of their families may be more likely to be referred to particular clinics for assessment.

The prognosis for growth is therefore good and many adolescents with CDGP may be reassured after explanation that their growth and development will proceed normally and final height will be within the normal range. Adolescence, however, encompasses more than just the physical changes of puberty but also includes psychological adjustment to adult life. Psychological distress at this time may be crucial for adjustment and personality development,[54-56] and may even persist into adult life.[57] In a recent retrospective study of untreated boys followed to final adult height, there was evidence of significant psychological distress in adolescence and a strong desire from the boys themselves for active treatment although in some cases attendance at clinic had provided some reassurance.[52] Further support for active intervention to advance the timing of puberty and growth was provided in a recent report which identified osteopenia in adult men with a history of CDGP who had not received any treatment.[58]

The aim of treatment in CDGP is to minimise the discrepancies in growth and development between the subject and his peers (Fig 5). In those presenting with short stature, this means advancing the timing of the growth spurt. In taller boys the main concern may be lack of virilisation. In either case it is essential that

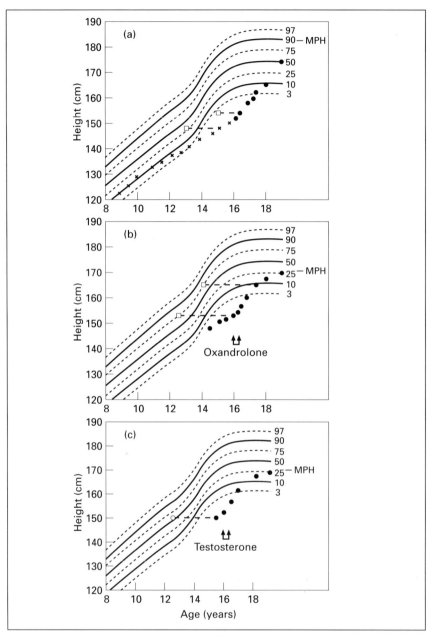

Fig 5. *Growth charts of three boys with CDGP presenting in early puberty (testicular volumes 4–6 ml): (a) did not receive any treatment and ended up with a final height on the 50th percentile; (b) received treatment with oxandrolone 2.5 mg daily for 3 months in early puberty and subsequently had a growth spurt at an earlier stage of puberty (testicular volumes 6 ml) than normal and ended up with an adult height on the 25th centile; (c) received testosterone intramuscularly monthly for 4 months and also had an earlier growth spurt (testicular volumes 6 ml) and ended up with an adult height at the mid-parental height (MPH)*

treatment is not at the expense of an inappropriate advance in skeletal maturation that would compromise final height. Once the decision has been made that treatment is indicated in a boy with CDGP, although there are several treatment options, short courses of cheap, simple treatments such as testosterone or oxandrolone would seem to be preferable, and administration to boys in early puberty has been shown to be successful in advancing the timing of growth. The growth response is determined by the degree of activation of the pituitary–testicular axis as reflected in circulating LH levels and testicular size, and not GH levels at the initiation of treatment.[59] Boys in the very early stages of puberty may therefore require a longer course of treatment to get the same growth effect.

Oxandrolone is a testosterone derivative with high anabolic but low androgenic activity.[60] Clinically, it is prescribed at low dose (1.25–2.5 mg daily) over a short course (3–6 months) for those boys whose complaint is principally short stature. In this dosage it has been shown to advance the timing of the growth spurt without excessive advance in skeletal age.[61] Growth is stimulated for the duration of treatment and then maintained for a variable period of time.[62,63] Final adult height is not affected either in children treated prepubertally for one year with low dose oxandrolone,[64] or in those treated at various pubertal stages for shorter periods of time.[65] Alternatively in boys who are primarily concerned about the slow advance of their pubertal development testosterone, usually testosterone enanthate, can be given 4 weekly as an intramuscular injection of 50 mg initially for 3 to 6 months, and again this treatment does not affect final height.[66] Low dose oestrogen can also be given to the girls who present with CDGP, although this is a rare problem

Conclusions

The endocrine changes of puberty result in dramatic gains in height, changes in body composition and the development of secondary sexual characteristics. Pulsatile secretion of GnRH stimulates pulsatile gonadotrophin secretion which stimulates the gonads to produce sex steroids and through oestrogen priming an increase in GH secretion. There are remarkable variations in the timing of both male and female puberty, although the sequence of changes is essentially constant. Nutrition is an important regulator of growth, and any chronic disease may affect the timing and tempo of growth and pubertal development. In addition significant specific pathologies may present as early or late puberty, necessitating careful assessment of these children. Nevertheless, the majority of children presenting with early or late puberty represent the extremes of the normal variation in the timing of puberty and often there is a family history of a similar pattern of development. Careful assessment is still essential, both to make the correct diagnosis and to assess the psychological impact of either early or late development and growth. In the former treatment with GnRH analogues, and in the latter with sex steroids may be indicated. The aim in both situations is to maintain peer group progress and optimise growth potential.

References

1. Tanner JM, Whitehouse RH. Clinical longitudinal standards for height, weight, height velocity, weight velocity and stages of puberty. *Archives of Disease in Childhood* 1976; **51**: 170–9.
2. Tanner JM, Whitehouse RH, Marubini E, Resele LF. The adolescent growth spurt of boys and girls of the Harpenden Growth Study. *Annals of Human Biology* 1976; **3**: 109–26.
3. Eveleth PB. Population differences in growth. In: *Human growth: a comprehensive treatise*. 2nd edn. New York, London: Plenum Press, 1986; 221–39.
4. Freeman JV, Cole TJ, Chinn S, Jones PRM, White EM, Preece MA. Cross sectional stature and weight reference curves for the UK, 1990. *Archives of Disease in Childhood* 1995; **73**: 17–24.
5. Garn SM, Clark DC. Nutrition, growth, development, and maturation: findings from the ten-state nutrition survey of 1968–70. *Pediatrics* 1975; **56**: 306–19.
6. Buckler J. *A longitudinal study of adolescent growth*. London: Springer-Verlag, 1990.
7. Mills JL, Shiono PH, Shapiro LR, Crawford PB, Rhoads GG. Early growth predicts timing of puberty in boys: results of a 14-year nutrition and growth study. *Journal of Pediatrics* 1986; **109**: 543–7.
8. Marti-Henneberg C, Vizmanos B, Moreno A, Cliville R, Altes A, Gens M, Morillo S, Ramiro O, Fernandez-Ballart J. Tempo of puberty and final height in boys. *Hormone Research* 1995; **44**: 5.
9. Bourguignon J-P. Linear growth as a function of age at onset of puberty and sex steroid dosage: therapeutic implications. *Endocrine Reviews* 1988; **9**: 467–88.
10. Burger HG, Yamada Y, Bangah ML, McCloud PI, Warne GL. Serum gonadotrophin, sex steroid, and immunoreactive inhibin levels in the first two years of life. *Journal of Clinical Endocrinology and Metabolism* 1991; **72**: 682–6.
11. Jakacki RI, Kelch RP, Sauder SE, Lloyd JS, Hopwood NJ, Marshall JC. Pulsatile secretion of luteinizing hormone in children. *Journal of Clinical Endocrinology and Metabolism* 1982; **55**: 453–8.
12. Wu FCW, Butler GE, Kelnar CJH, Stirling HF, Huhtaniemi I. Patterns of pulsatile luteinizing hormone and follicle-stimulating hormone secretion in prepubertal (midchildhood) boys and girls and patients with

idiopathic hypogonadotropic hypogonadism (Kallmann's Syndrome): a study using an ultrasensitive time-resolved immunofluorometric assay. *Journal of Clinical Endocrinology and Metabolism* 1991; **72**: 1229–37.

13. Hale PM, Khoury S, Foster CM, Beitins IZ, Hopwood NJ, Marshall JC, Kelch RP. Increased luteinizing hormone pulse frequency during sleep in early to midpubertal boys: effects of testosterone infusion. *Journal of Clinical Endocrinology and Metabolism* 1988; **66**: 785–91.

14. Wennink JMB, Delamerre-van de Waal HA, Schoemaker R, Schoemaker H, Schoemaker J. Luteinizing hormone and follicle stimulating hormone secretion patterns in boys throughout puberty measured using highly sensitive immunoradiometric assays. *Clinical Endocrinology* 1989; **31**: 551–64.

15. Wu FCW, Borrow SM, Nicol K, Elton R, Hunter WM. Ontogeny of pulsatile gonadotrophin secretion and pituitary responsiveness in male puberty in man: a mixed longitudinal and cross-sectional study. *Journal of Endocrinology* 1989; **123**: 347–59.

16. Lucky AW, Rich BH, Rosenfield RL, Fang VS, Roche-Bender N. LH bioactivity increases more than immunoreactivity during puberty. *Journal of Pediatrics* 1980; **97**: 205–13.

17. Reiter EO, Beitins IZ, Ostrea T, Gutai JP. Bioassayable luteinizing hormone during childhood and adolescence and in patients with delayed pubertal development. *Journal of Clinical Endocrinology and Metabolism* 1982; **54**: 155–61.

18. Rich BH, Rosenfield RL, Moll GW, Lucky AW, Roche-Bender N, Fang V. Bioactive luteinizing hormone pituitary reserves during normal and abnormal male puberty. *Journal of Clinical Endocrinology and Metabolism* 1982; **55**: 140–6.

19. Dunger DB, Villa AK, Matthews DR, Edge JA, Jones J, Rothwell C, Preece MA, Robertson WR. Pattern of secretion of bioactive and immunoreactive gonadotrophins in normal pubertal children. *Clinical Endocrinology* 1991; **35**: 267–75.

20. Holly JMP, Smith CP, Dunger DB, Howell RJS, Chard T, Perry LA, Savage MO, Cianfarani S, Rees LH, Wass JAH. Relationship between the pubertal fall in sex hormone binding globulin and insulin-like growth factor binding protein-1. A synchronized approach to pubertal development? *Clinical Endocrinology* 1989; **31**: 277–84.

21. Foster CM, Hassing JM, Mendes TM, Hale PM, Padmanabhan V, Hopwood NJ, Beitins IZ, Marshall JC, Kelch RP. Testosterone infusion reduces nocturnal luteinizing hormone pulse frequency in pubertal boys. *Journal of Clinical Endocrinology and Metabolism* 1989; **69**: 1213–20.

22. Reiter EO, Kulin HE, Hamwood SM. The absence of positive feedback between estrogen and luteinizing hormone in sexually immature girls. *Pediatric Research* 1974; **8**: 740–5.

23. Mauras N, Blizzard RM, Link K, Johnson ML, Rogol AD, Veldhuis JD. Augmentation of growth hormone secretion during puberty: evidence for a pulse amplitude-modulated phenomenon. *Journal of Clinical Endocrinology and Metabolism* 1987; **64**: 596–601.

24. Martha PM, Rogol AD, Veldhuis JD, Kerrigan JR, Goodman DW, Blizzard RM. Alterations in the pulsatile properties of circulating growth hormone concentrations during puberty in boys. *Journal of Clinical Endocrinology and Metabolism* 1989; **69**: 563–70.

25. Rose SR, Municchi G, Barnes KM, Kamp GA, Uriarte MM, Ross JL, Cassoria F, Cutler GB. Spontaneous growth hormone secretion increases during puberty in normal boys and girls. *Journal of Clinical Endocrinology and Metabolism* 1991; **73**: 428–35.
26. Aynsley-Green A, Zachman M, Prader A. Interrelation of the therapeutic effects of growth hormone and testosterone on growth in hypopituitarism. *Journal of Pediatrics* 1976; **89**: 992–9.
27. Zachman M, Prader A. Anabolic and androgenic effect of testosterone in sexually immature boys and its dependency on growth hormone. *Journal of Clinical Endocrinology and Metabolism* 1970; **30**: 85.
28. Martin LG, Clark JW, Connor TB. Growth hormone secretion enhanced by androgens. *Journal of Clinical Endocrinology and Metabolism* 1968; **28**: 425–8.
29. Sperling MA, Kenny FM, Drash AL. Arginine-induced growth hormone responses in children: effect of age and puberty. *Journal of Pediatrics* 1970; **77**: 462–5.
30. Liu L, Merriam GR, Sherins RJ. Chronic sex steroid exposure increases mean plasma growth hormone concentration and pulse amplitude in men with isolated hypogonadotrophic hypogonadism. *Journal of Clinical Endocrinology and Metabolism* 1987; **64**: 651–6.
31. Stanhope R, Pringle PJ, Brook CGD. The mechanism of the adolescent growth spurt induced by low dose pulsatile GnRH treatment. *Clinical Endocrinology* 1988; **28**: 83–91.
32. Ross JL, Pescovitz OH, Barnes K, Loriaux DL, Cutler GB. Growth hormone secretory dynamics in children with precocious puberty. *Journal of Pediatrics* 1987; **110**: 369–72.
33. Stanhope R, Pringle PJ, Brook CGD. Growth, growth hormone and sex steroid secretion in girls with central precocious puberty treated with a gonadotrophin releasing hormone (GnRH) analogue. *Acta Paediatrica Scandinavica* 1988; **77**: 525–30.
34. Ho KY, Evans WS, Blizzard RM, Veldhuis JD, Merriam GR, Samojlik E, Furlanetto R, Rogol AD, Kaiser DL, Thorner MO. Effects of sex and age on the 24-hour profile of growth hormone secretion in man: importance of endogenous estradiol concentrations. *Journal of Clinical Endocrinology and Metabolism* 1987; **64**: 51–8.
35. Caruso-Nicoletti M, Cassorla F, Skerda M, Ross JL, Loriaux DL, Cutler GB. Short term, low dose estradiol accelerates ulnar growth in boys. *Journal of Clinical Endocrinology and Metabolism* 1985; **61**: 896–8.
36. Moll GW, Rosenfield RL, Fang VS. Administration of low-dose estrogen rapidly and directly stimulates growth hormone production. *American Journal of Diseases of Children* 1986; **140**: 124–7.
37. Metzger DL, Kerrigan JR. Androgen receptor blockade with flutamide enhances growth hormone secretion in late pubertal males: evidence for independent actions of estrogen and androgen. *Journal of Clinical Endocrinology and Metabolism* 1993; **76**: 1147–52.
38. Zachman M, Prader A, Sobel E, Crigler JF, Ritzen EM, Atares M, Fernandez A. Pubertal growth in patients with androgen insensitivity: indirect evidence for the importance of estrogens in pubertal growth of girls. *Journal of Pediatrics* 1986; **108**: 694–7.
39. Pescovitz OH. The endocrinology of the pubertal growth spurt. *Acta Paediatrica Scandinavica* 1990; **367**: 37.

40. Smith CP, Archibald HR, Thomas JM, Tarn AC, Williams AJK, Gale EAM, Savage MO. Basal and stimulated insulin levels rise with advancing puberty. *Clinical Endocrinology* 1988; **28**: 7–14.

41. Amiel SA, Caprio S, Sherwin RS, Plewe G, Haymond MW, Tamborlane WV. Insulin resistance of puberty: a defect restricted to peripheral glucose metabolism. *Journal of Clinical Endocrinology and Metabolism* 1991; **72**: 277–82.

42. Holly JMP, Smith CP, Dunger DB, Edge JA, Biddlecombe RA, Williams AJK, Howell R, Chard T, Savage MO, Rees LH, Wass JAH. Levels of the small insulin-like growth factor-binding protein are strongly related to those of insulin in prepubertal and pubertal children but only weakly so after puberty. *Journal of Endocrinology* 1989; **121**: 383–7.

43. Taylor AM, Dunger DB, Preece MA, Holly JMP, Smith CP, Wass JAH, Patelo S, Tate VE. The growth hormone independent insulin-like growth factor-I binding protein BP-28 is associated with serum insulin-like growth factor-I inhibitory bioactivity in adolescent insulin-dependent diabetics. *Clinical Endocrinology* 1990; **32**: 229–39.

44. Stanhope R, Brook CGD. Thelarche variant: a new syndrome of precocious sexual development? *Acta Endocrinologica* 1990; **123**: 481–6.

45. Stanhope R, Adams J, Brook CGD. The treatment of central precocious puberty using an intranasal LHRH analogue (Buserelin). *Clinical Endocrinology* 1985; **22**: 795–806.

46. Oerter KE, Manasco P, Barnes KM, Jones J, Hill S, Cutler GB. Adult height after long term treatment with deslorelin. *Journal of Clinical Endocrinology and Metabolism* 1991; **73**: 1235–40.

47. Partsch CJ, Oostdijk W, Albers N, Drop SLS, Sippell WG. Combined treatment with a depot GnRH agonist and GH in girls with central precocious puberty (CPP) and low height velocity: effects on growth and bone maturation. *Hormone Research* 1995; **44**: 37.

48. Levine MA. The McCune–Albright syndrome: the whys and wherefores of abnormal signal transduction. *New England Journal of Medicine* 1991; **325**: 1738–40.

49. Shenker A, Laue L, Kosugi S, Merendino JJ Jr, Minegishi T, Cutler GB. A constitutively activating mutation of the luteinizing hormone receptor in familial male precocious puberty. *Nature* 1993; **365**: 652–4.

50. Gourmelen M, Pham-Huu-Trung MT, Girard F. Transient partial hGH deficiency in prepubertal children with delay of growth. *Pediatric Research* 1979; **13**: 221–4.

51. LaFranchi S, Hanna CE, Mandel SH. Constitutional delay of growth. Expected versus adult height. *Pediatrics* 1991; **87**: 82–7.

52. Crowne EC, Shalet SM, Wallace WHB, Eminson D, Price DA. Final height in boys with untreated constitutional delay in growth and puberty (CDGP). *Archives of Disease in Childhood* 1990; **65**: 1109–12.

53. Kalckreuth G, Haverkamp F, Kessler M, Rosskamp RH. Constitutional delay of growth and puberty: do they really reach their target height? *Hormone Research* 1991; **35**: 222–5.

54. Mussen PH, Jones MC. Selfconceptions, motivations and interpersonal attitudes of late and early maturing boys. *Child Development* 1957; **28**: 243–56.

55. Duke PM, Carlsmith JM, Jennings D, Martin JA, Dornbusch SM, Gross RT, Siegel-Gorelick B. Educational correlates of early and late sexual maturation in adolescence. *Journal of Pediatrics* 1982; **100**: 633–7.

56. Gordon M, Crouthamel C, Post EM, Richman RA. Psychosocial aspects of constitutional short stature: social competence, behaviour problems, self-esteem and family functioning. *Journal of Pediatrics* 1982; **101**: 477–80.

57. Jones MC. The later careers of boys who were early- or late-maturing. *Child Development* 1957; **28**: 113–28.

58. Finkelstein JS, Neer RM, Biller BMK, Crawford JD, Klibanski A. Osteopenia in men with a history of delayed puberty. *New England Journal of Medicine* 1992; **326**: 600–4.

59. Crowne EC, Wallace WHB, Moore C, Mitchell R, Robertson WR, Shalet SM. Degree of activation of the pituitary–testicular axis in early pubertal boys with constitutional delay of growth and puberty (CDGP) determines the growth response to treatment with testosterone or oxandrolone. *Journal of Clinical Endocrinology and Metabolism* 1995; **80**: 1869–75.

60. Fox M, Minot AS, Liddle GW. Oxandrolone: a potent anabolic steroid of novel chemical configuration. *Journal of Clinical Endocrinology and Metabolism* 1962; **22**: 921–4.

61. Stanhope R, Brook CGD. Oxandrolone in low dose for constitutional delay of growth and puberty in boys. *Archives of Disease in Childhood* 1985; **60**: 379–81.

62. Marti-Henneberg C, Niirianen AK, Rappaport R. Oxandrolone treatment of constitutional short stature in boys during adolescence: effect on linear growth, bone age, pubic hair, and testicular development. *Journal of Pediatrics* 1975; **86**: 783–8.

63. Clayton PE, Shalet SM, Price DA, Addison GM. Growth and growth hormone responses to oxandrolone in boys with constitutional delay in growth and puberty (CDGP). *Clinical Endocrinology* 1988; **29**: 123–30.

64. Joss EE, Schmidt HA, Zuppinger KA. Oxandrolone in constitutionally delayed growth: a longitudinal study up to final height. *Journal of Clinical Endocrinology and Metabolism* 1989; **69**: 1109–15.

65. Tse W-Y, Buyukgebiz A, Hindmarsh PC, Stanhope R, Preece MA, Brook CGD. Long-term outcome of oxandrolone treatment in boys with constitutional delay of growth and puberty. *Journal of Pediatrics* 1990; **117**: 588–91.

66. Uruena M, Pantsiotou S, Preece MA, Stanhope R. Is testosterone therapy for boys with constitutional delay of growth and puberty associated with impaired final height and suppression of the hypothalamic–pituitary–gonadal axis? *European Journal of Pediatrics* 1992; **151**: 15–18.

67. Marshall WA, Tanner JM. Variations in the pattern of pubertal changes in boys. *Archives of Disease in Childhood* 1970; **45**: 13–23.

9 The adolescent with diabetes

Stephen Greene
*Consultant in Paediatric Endocrinology, Ninewells Hospital,
Dundee*

Insulin-dependent diabetes mellitus (IDDM) is a relatively common organic illness which occurs in adolescence. The peak incidence of presentation for IDDM is around 10–12 years of age. Currently in the United Kingdom the incidence is around 20–25/100,000 16 year olds[1] with a prevalence of 1.4/100,000 16 year olds.[2] Twenty-five per cent of children present with diabetes under the age of 5 years and consequently many adolescents with IDDM have had the disease for some considerable time. The average district general hospital, therefore, in the United Kingdom is likely to have between 60 and 100 diabetic children and teenagers under its care with the majority of these subjects being in their teenage years. This appears to be the single biggest specific metabolic disease in this age group likely to require medical care in a health district.

Adolescents with IDDM are viewed with concern by health professionals. The majority of diabetic adolescents, however, maintain excellent health throughout their teenage years developing physically at the normal rate and requiring no special health care provision other than for any child or adult with diabetes. However, adolescence is also a period of extreme difficulty with diabetes and a small number of teenagers (not necessarily always a constant group) can go through a difficult period of metabolic control with the early development of microvascular complications. The ability to cope with the diabetes at this age period is often troublesome and sometimes disastrous.

Blood glucose control and adolescence

There undoubtedly is a deterioration in blood glucose control as children pass into the teenage years. The mean glycosylated haemoglobin level (HbA1c) in the children attending our clinic at

97

Dundee ranges from 7.6 to 8.4% throughout a year. Throughout the similar period in the teenagers (12 to 21) HbA1c levels vary from 8.5 to 9.6%. While in both groups there is a skewed distribution of glycosylated haemoglobin with some children and teenagers having extremely poor metabolic control, there does appear to be an over-all deterioration in blood glucose control with this average rise in 1% of HbA1c values. This deterioration appears secondary to sever-al factors including physiological changes, lifestyle changes, and in some cases non-adherence to diabetes routine.

Physiological changes of glucose metabolism in adolescence are seen in normal subjects. There does appear to be an increasing insulin 'resistance' and this can be reflected in change in fasting insulin levels moving from childhood into puberty.[3] There are also major changes in the insulin-like growth factor 1 (IGF-1) binding protein and growth hormone concentration in association with the pubertal growth spurt.[4] Body composition changes with an increase in the percentage body fat reflecting both the insulin resistance and hormonal changes in puberty, although it may in itself also relate to a change in glucose metabolism. These physio-logical changes in glucose metabolism appear to be heightened in adolescents with IDDM. There appears to be a need for an increase in insulin dosage to maintain a similar level of glycaemia moving from childhood to adolescence. Insulin-like growth factor 1 decreases significantly in the pubertal years and there are major increases in IGF binding protein and growth hormone concentra-tion.[4] Body composition changes can be quite marked in teenagers with diabetes, particularly in females (see Fig 1).[5]

Complications of diabetes in adolescence

The main complications of diabetes are hypoglycaemia, diabetic ketoacidosis and the development of micro- and macro-vascular disease.

Hypoglycaemia is unfortunately a reasonably common experi-ence for many teenagers with diabetes. Severe episodes (that is, hypoglycaemia requiring assistance with or without the develop-ment of coma) occur in approximately 30% of teenagers and are recurrent in 20% of subjects, with 30% of hypos occurring at night. Sudden unexpected death in adolescence is a rare occur-rence and is probably related to hypoglycaemia. Many of these tragic episodes occur at night. There is often a period of unstable blood glucose control prior to the episode and alcohol ingestion has been implicated in many of the episodes. There has recently

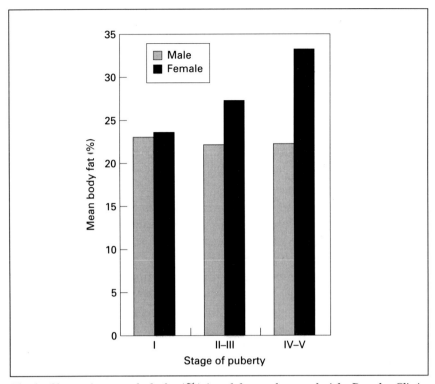

Fig 1. *Change in mean body fat (%) in adolescent boys and girls, Dundee Clinic. Body fat measured by skin fold thickness. Normal mean: adolescent women 24%; adolescent men 19%*

been a debate on the role of human insulin in this problem but the evidence as such at the moment is fairly slim and the British Diabetic Association does not recommend changing from human insulin preparations unless the patient specifically requests this.[6]

Diabetic ketoacidosis in adolescence again is a rare phenomenon although some teenagers appear to be affected severely by this problem. This group are often placed under the label of 'brittle diabetes'. These subjects tend to be in their adolescent period or early adulthood. They have frequent episodes of unexplained diabetic ketoacidosis. The majority are female, slightly overweight and possibly over-treated with insulin. Some undoubtedly have an overt psychiatric or psychological illness. However, after many years of investigations no underlying biochemical or physiological abnormality has been detected. This group are undoubtedly at the extreme end of the vast majority of teenagers who present with diabetic ketoacidosis who are overtly or subconsciously manipulating their diabetes. Recent data from our clinic could find no specific

Table 1. Early changes of vascular disease in adolescents with IDDM

- Microalbuminuria
- Cardiovascular autonomic neuropathy
- Sensory nerve damage
- Retinopathy
- Cheirarthropathy
- Skin vascular changes
- Vascular endothelial pathology

reason for the vast majority of young people being admitted with diabetic ketoacidosis and certainly no evidence that there was any underlying infection. This contrasts sharply with the middle aged adult who presents with diabetic ketoacidosis.

The early changes of vascular disease in puberty can be detected by a series of biophysical investigations.[7] Very few teenagers exhibit any symptoms of overt microvascular disease although severe retinopathy and nephropathy together with autonomic neuropathy have been described in some young people. Puberty appears to accelerate the various microvascular changes with for instance 15–20% of young people having microalbuminuria by the age of 20 (Table 1). Of significance also is the probable development of the antecedents of macrovascular disease in adolescence with signs of abnormal vascular flow and markers of endothelial damage. These changes eventually progress, accounting for the excessive mortality in young adults in their 30s and 40s with IDDM. Standardised mortality rates suggest that the incidence of coronary artery disease and strokes is approximately 3–4 times higher in males with greater than 8 times the standard mortality rate seen in young women.

Coping with diabetes in adolescence

The period of adolescence is regarded as a period of change for the whole population, starting with the onset of puberty, through to about 16–18 years. This change often appears to play havoc with diabetes control and the ability to cope with the management of diabetes which in itself is influenced by family functioning as well as the knowledge of diabetes and the acceptance of the diabetes routine.

Undoubtedly teenagers in a stable family background with involved and caring parents and siblings find life much easier than

Table 2. Chaotic diabetic control during adolescence

- Binge eating
- Missing insulin injections
- Fear of hypoglycaemia
- Failed crisis management
- Over insulinisation
- Alcohol excess
- 'Brittle diabetes'

those in disrupted families and families with major, and even minor, emotional difficulties. Severe difficulties with diabetic control can be seen in children with parents going through divorce or with families ravaged by alcoholism or other drug addiction problems.

Knowledge itself of diabetes (ie understanding of the pathophysiology together with the practical aspects of insulin therapy and dietary control) does not in itself necessarily produce good control. However, lack of knowledge of diabetes, particularly in practical aspects of the giving of insulin, management of diabetic crises and the maintaining of a good diabetes routine, undoubtedly does produce poor control.

Many teenagers go through a period of chaos in relation to their diabetic control during adolescence. This erratic blood glucose control in association with frequent symptoms of hypoglycaemia and admission for ketoacidosis are often related to fairly practical misdemeanours which are outlined in Table 2. Most teenagers experience periods of difficulty with their diabetes although it is only a few who persist with the problems leading to chaotic metabolic control.

Strategies for management

Undoubtedly teenagers with diabetes have to be taken as a special case. To this end, they require both a different clinical approach and special facilities.

Adolescent diabetics have to be approached against the background of normal adolescence. Specific difficulties leading to chaos have to be considered at all times, understood and helped where possible. Insulin therapy has to be adjusted appropriately and care has to be taken not to either underdose or, indeed, overdose the teenager with diabetes. Teenagers have to be counselled against the inappropriateness of missing insulin injections, particularly where this has resulted in diabetic ketoacidosis, a major life-threatening event.

Multiple injection therapy (ie pre-meal soluble insulin with a pre-evening isophane type preparation) has over the years been suggested as good therapy for teenagers. However, the evidence that this improves overall control is limited. Recently the Diabetes Control and Complication Trial (DCCT) in the United States produced overwhelming evidence that good blood glucose control sustained over many years prevents the onset of diabetic microvascular disease.[8] We, therefore, have to aim for the best possible blood glucose control and it appears from this study that multiple injection therapy or pump insulin therapy is the desired option. However, these were highly selected and self-motivated patients supported in the field to a major extent by diabetic counsellors. The use of multiple injection therapy in the clinical setting without an input of major clinical support has proved less successful and, indeed, evidence from Denmark suggests that teenagers who are just given multiple injection therapy as part of their everyday diabetes treatment have the same problems of deteriorating blood glucose control and increasing obesity as all teenagers with diabetes. Use of the multiple injection insulin regimen to achieve good blood glucose control aiming at a glycosylated haemoglobin of 7% or less requires considerable effort from the teenager with adherence to a regular routine and dietary intake.

New drug therapy will undoubtedly be available for teenagers with diabetes in the near future. Insulin-like growth factor 1 has appeal given its deficiency during the pubertal years and trials are currently being established for its use as an adjunct to insulin therapy, particularly for use during the night.[9] Drugs used to prevent microvascular complications are already part of the diabetes care package with vigorous attempts to reduce hypertension, particularly in young teenagers with evidence of microalbuminuria. Other drugs undoubtedly will become available over the next few years, particularly in relation to the development of macrovascular complications.

The young adult clinic

Given the special case outlined for young people with diabetes, there is a strong case for a special facility being required for provision of their service. A young adult clinic has been established in many forms in many centres throughout the United Kingdom. They need to be attractive to teenagers and care has to be taken concerning their style, venue and timing. They almost certainly should be joint, ie there should be involvement from the paediatric team as well as the adult diabetic team. This has to be discussed between the various teams as to the best use of each other's time as, in my experience, young adult clinics to be successful need to be labour intensive. The clinic has to be concerned with the screening for microvascular disease, particularly in relation to blood pressure and hypertension.

Special advice needs to be given on the dangers of smoking, excessive alcohol use and potential problems with other drugs. Of major importance for young girls is pre-pregnancy advice in an attempt to reduce potential physical complications of conception during a period of poor diabetic control.

Finally, all services involved with insulin-dependent diabetes require to know the extent of their problem and it is mandatory that a local register exists of all diabetic patients. It is imperative that defaulters from the clinical service during the adolescent period are identified given the major risk to these patients of developing the severe and life-threatening complications of diabetes in their early adult years.

References

1. Metcalfe MA, Baum JD. Incidence of insulin dependent diabetes in children aged under 15 years in the British Isles during 1988. *British Medical Journal* 1991; **302**: 443–7.
2. Smail P. (Personal Data). Presentation at the Scottish Study Group for the Care of the Young Diabetic, October 1993.
3. Hindmarsh PC, Matthews DR, Silvio LDI, Kurtz AB, Brook CGD. Relation between height velocity and fasting insulin concentrations. *Archives of Disease in Childhood* 1988; **63**: 665–6.
4. Dunger DB, Cheetham TD. The adolescent with diabetes. *Current Paediatrics* 1993; **3**: 125–9.
5. Gregory JW, Wilson AC, Greene SA. Obesity among adolescents with diabetes. *Diabetic Medicine* 1992; **9**: 344–7.
6. Tattersall R, Gill G. Unexplained deaths of type 1 diabetic patients. *Diabetic Medicine* 1991; **8**: 49–58.
7. Greene SA. Diabetes mellitus in childhood and adolescence. In: Pickup J, Williams G (eds). *Textbook of Diabetes*. Oxford: Blackwell Scientific Publications, 1991.
8. The Diabetes Control and Complication Trial Research Group. The effect of intensive treatment of diabetes on the development and progression of long-term complications in insulin dependent diabetes mellitus. *New England Journal of Medicine* 1993; **329**: 977–86.
9. Dunger DB, Cheetham TD, Holly JMP, Matthews DR. Does recombinant insulin-like growth factor I have a role in the treatment of insulin-dependent diabetes mellitus during adolescence? *Acta Paediatrica* Suppl 1993 Mar; **388**: 49–52.

10 | The skin in adolescence

Terence J Ryan
Clinical Professor of Dermatology, The Churchill Hospital, Oxford

The functions of the skin include display, thermoregulation, protection and sensory perception.[1] Skin failure when any of these functions is impaired gives rise to considerable disability.[2] The adolescent is particularly vulnerable to the effects of his or her failure to display. Skin is an organ of communication depicted by such terms as 'love at first sight' or 'colour prejudice', and in making friends, mating, or going for an interview for a job, if as a teenager one is to succeed, one needs not only to look good but to feel good. In this chapter six problems affecting the adolescent skin are discussed to illustrate certain themes which should be understood in the management of skin disease of young people.

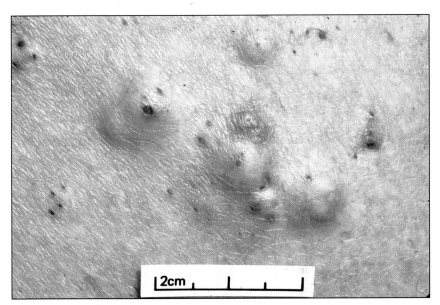

Fig 1. *Comedones and cysts contributing to the disfigurement of acne*

Acne vulgaris

Acne vulgaris[3] is especially a disorder of adolescence (Fig 1). The cause is enhanced activity of the sebaceous apparatus in response to male sex hormones. Keratinisation of the excretory duct and increased sebum secretion combine to obstruct the apparatus, and bacteria residing in the skin produce inflammatory agents which result in the pustular phase of acne. The combination is an obstruction at the surface known as a blackhead or comedone as well as a slightly deeper obstruction in the skin, known as a whitehead. It is followed by a dilated or cystic swelling with white cell infiltration and damage to the sebaceous apparatus as well as to the surrounding dermis. The end result can be very disfiguring as it is both inflammatory and scarring. Apart from the irritation and pain of such lesions, the large pustules and cystic swellings are usually unsightly, and those affected have considerable loss of confidence in their appearance. They find interviews and social gatherings difficult to handle.[4] There is a hidden agenda too which may suggest that the beautiful are good and successful, but the ugly or scar-faced are wicked (Fig 2).

Acne vulgaris is for the most part completely controllable and curable. There is no justification for ignoring it or for not treating it effectively. Unfortunately, acne is not always taken seriously by physicians and contemporary funding of the NHS may opt not to fund the adequate treatment of acne.

Fig 2. *The contribution of how one looks to how one feels is well documented: the disfigured are often misjudged.* (Dr David DeBerker for British Association of Dermatology brochure)

Mild acne responds to over-the-counter preparations, which often have a peeling effect, thereby unplugging the blackheads. They reduce sebum secretion and the activity of bacteria. Antibiotics such as tetracyclines are often effective in controlling acne. The hormonal pathogenesis of acne is controlled often very well in the female by prescribing anti-androgens in the form of the contraceptive Dianette.

There is a small percentage of adolescents whose acne is resistant to the above described therapy. The management of this group has been revolutionised by Roaccutane.[5] The prescription of Roaccutane in the dose 1 mg/kg for 4 months shrivels up the inflamed sebaceous apparatus and restores the skin to a completely cosmetically acceptable state and protects against ultimate scarring. At present it is a hospital only prescription, and many dermatology departments are finding that for relatively few patients this expensive drug is taking more than 50% of their entire pharmacy budget. Strong arguments can be provided in favour of prescription:

1. Using a range of disability analysis systems, these patients can be shown to be severely disabled.
2. Evidence-based medicine can be invoked to prove the effectiveness of the drug in its complete relief of disability.
3. The cost of a 4 month course of this effective therapy is less than the prolonged courses of other drugs that may be given for several years.[6]

Unfortunately many purchasers are not persuaded that acne is important and impose unwarranted restrictions on the prescribing of the drug.

Blushing

Blushing and flushing can be a problem for the self-conscious adolescent. It is brought on by exercise, heating or emotion. Vasolability is a variable feature in this age group and the consequences of flushing include a bright red face, sweating and, in some teenagers, cholinergic urticaria. This latter is a small wheal lasting some 10 or so minutes acccompanied by the flush. It stings rather than itches. It affects the face and upper half of the body. The problem of blushing and of cholinergic urticaria is mostly noticeable when stripped of clothing in, for instance, the changing room, but it may occur at social occasions such as at a dance or when sitting in front of a mirror while having a haircut.

The management of flushing includes avoiding known causes,

such as eating foods which are heated or spicy, or drinking alcoholic beverages when this is found to induce flushing. Cholinergic urticaria responds to Atarax in a dose which can be judged between 10 mg and 25 mg once, twice or three times daily. There is a variable response which includes sedation in a range from no sleepiness to being 'knocked out'. Flushing may be reduced by beta blockers, or by reduction in clothing and other causes of overheating. Overheating at night due to contemporary bed clothing and room temperatures is believed by some dermatologists to contribute to flushing.[7] Mostly counselling is all that is required, an explanation that it is common and physiological, assuaging the feeling of embarrassment and anxiety which is so upsetting. Hypnosis can be used as an anxiety suppressor. Sipping iced water reduces gustatory flushing. Disease-associated causes of flushing are mostly not seen in the adolescent.

Sweating and stress-related disorders of the foot

Sweating of the feet and of the hands, face and axillae is a common problem in adolescence. It is strongly induced by anxiety but it is also a normal activity of the skin. The commonest problem of excess sweating is almost entirely a consequence of footwear. The young are energetic and mobile on their feet. The soles and sides of the feet take considerable shearing stresses when running, especially in confined areas requiring sudden changes in direction, as in the playground or on the squash court. Sweat, to some extent, encourages surface friction and is an advantage in some activities which require firm contact between the hand and foot and its environment. It is often pointed out that the monkey climbing a tree would be handicapped by a dry palm and sole, since gripping is enhanced by sweating. In the shoe, a wet foot gives rise to a friction dermatitis of the forefoot (Fig 3). It is commoner in those using modern footwear with plasticised insoles, and it is compounded by artificial fibre socks in which there is little absorption of sweat. The red, sweating foot, shoe and sock are host to bacteria, which produce strong odours. 'Smelly feet' are common in the adolescent. The management includes wearing of sandals, cotton socks or odour-absorbing insoles, aerating the shoe even by making holes in the side of the shoe to draw in air as the foot moves within the shoe. Normal hygiene, to encourage a clean bacteria-free foot, and the use of antiseptic agents or foot powders may be helpful. Contemporary surgical techniques for sympathectomy are so much safer than before that they should be

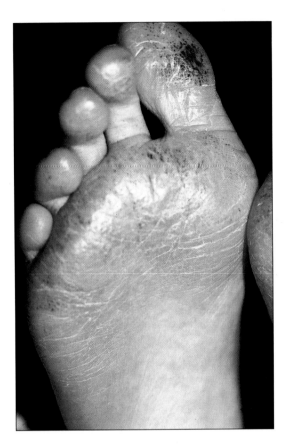

Fig 3. *The atopic forefoot showing the effects of a friction dermatitis, usually as a consequence of the atopic dry skin bathed in the sweat of a plastic non-absorbable sock and shoe*

considered seriously for adolescents who are severely disabled by sweating of the hands or feet. Nevertheless, the problem may be a transitory instability of adolescence and sympathectomy may have a permanent effect, so surgical management should not be entered into until all other systems have been tried. Aluminium salts are effective antiperspirants but they must be used according to instructions, which principally relate to applying the agents to a dried skin, otherwise they cause irritation.

Another consequence of mechanical stress on the foot is the 'ingrowing toenail'. This is mostly due to the pressure of the shoe on the outer soft tissues of the hallux major compressing the tissue at the edge of the nail. Adjustment of footwear so that the toecap is not narrow and there is no crowding of the toes, and sometimes surgery to remove the soft tissues or part of the offending nail, are skills commonly provided by a foot surgeon, dermatologist or podiatrist.[8]

In the 4th interdigital space, a soft corn may also develop over the head of the 4th metatarsal as a result of compression within a tight shoe. The verruca also favours sites of repetitive trauma and footwear adjustment is part of the routine of the podiatrist treating the plantar wart.

Atopic eczema

Eczema and dermatitis are interchangeable terms. There is a gradually increasing incidence of atopy affecting skin and lungs. The explanation is unclear but many refer to changes in the micro-climate of the house affecting the human frame or the house dust mite. There is also reference to environmental pollution and changes in the stimulus to the immune system as common para-sites and bacteria become less frequent invaders of the human body. Mostly atopic eczema is a problem of infants, and in only about 25% of cases is it still troublesome in the adolescent. The problem for the adolescent of managing the itch and scratch and the need for frequent anointing of the skin is not very different from that in other age groups. On the other hand, growing up and developing new relationships while reducing dependence on par-ents, can be more of a problem in the adolescent with atopic eczema. Because of the close bonding that tends to exist the anointing of the skin and the management of itch and scratch is a very 'physical' process, involving much contact with parents in early childhood. Touch is an important factor in bonding which should be released in adolescence.[9] No other condition so regular-ly brings both parents with the adolescent to the dermatology clin-ic. Sleep disturbance for parents and child often involves sharing of beds to a much later age than normal. The child feels very secure with his parents and receives much input from both of them. Hence, the child with atopy often seems more confident, extrovert and knowing. All this sometimes makes adolescence, with its complex changes in relationship, more difficult for the atopic, who may suffer from anxiety and a feeling of ineffectiveness.[10] The ritual of bathing and anointing with emollients has to continue, and the bathroom has to become a private rather than a public place often for the first time in adolescence. The management details are complex and are available in standard texts or from the National Eczema Society, 163 Eversholt Street, London NW1 1BU. Some treatments, like cyclosporin, are last resorts that can have an enormous benefit on the quality of life.[11] The cost to the individual of keeping the skin presentable is high for an age group that may be mostly unemployed.[12]

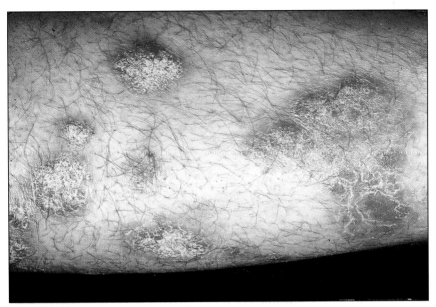

Fig 4. *Scale and redness illustrate psoriasis, which commonly presents in adolescence*

Psoriasis

Unlike atopic eczema which begins in infancy when bonding is strong, psoriasis often begins in adolescence when the bond is broken. A feeling of isolation and rejection[13] may be that much stronger when one is disfigured for the first time as a teenager. The scale and the redness (Fig 4) is uncomfortable and the affected person does not like to display it. Close body contact and touching are diminished. It is especially a cause of anxiety in a changing room or at the swimming bath. The peak age of onset of psoriasis is described as of genetic significance since there is an early onset with one pattern of inheritance, and a late onset with another. The development of psoriasis following a sore throat is a consequence of the sharing of skin antigens with the streptococcus. This too occurs quite commonly in adolescence for the first time. Psoriasis favours the scalp and control of dandruff can be a special cosmetic problem. Nevertheless, dermatology departments can offer effective therapy of psoriasis.[14] The Psoriasis Association (7 Milton Street, Northampton, NN2 7JG) provides social support and useful literature for all age groups.

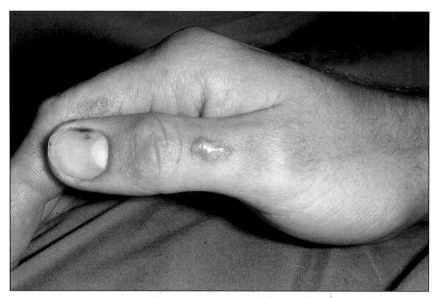

Fig 5. *A scar resulting from tattoo removal is often preferable to pornography or a tribal mark*

Tattooing

Tattoos are a common cause of referral to dermatology clinics. Mostly this is to request their removal in the age group 20–30, but the tattoos are acquired in early adolescence, and as such they are usually self-induced on exposed sites such as the hands and face, because they are for display. Peer pressures determine what is tattooed and they provide a tribal identity.[15] Mostly the tribal associations are no longer desired when an adult. The exception is the more respectable tattoo of the upper arm or trunk in the armed forces and other cultural groups.

Tattoos can be removed, though not without scarring. Some small tattoos on the back of the hand can be excised with minimal scarring but mostly larger tattoos are removed by burning and the consequent scars may be preferred because a burn has less tribal associations (Fig 5).

Acids, heat and cold are used. The lasers that have been introduced in the last decade are a great advance in tattoo management, but large professional tattoos are not possible to remove effectively by any technique. Mostly they are colourful and non-pornographic and are not on exposed sites. It is the amateur tattoo which most often needs to be removed, and the technology is now available. Unfortunately, the NHS does not always understand the value of such treatment. Removing a tattoo may be the means of introducing the subject into employment and into conforming with society. Not doing so can be expensive for society.

References

1. Ryan TJ. The naked survivor as manager. In: Weatherall DJ, Ledingham JDG, Warrell DA (eds) *Diseases of the Skin. Oxford Textbook of Medicine,* 3rd edition. Oxford University Press, 1995.
2. Ryan TJ. Disability in dermatology. *British Journal of Hospital Medicine* 1991; **46**: 33–6.
3. Ebling FJG, Cunliffe WJ. Disorders of the sebaceous glands. In: Champion RH, Burton JL, Ebling FJG (eds) *Rook, Wilkinson & Ebling Textbook of Dermatology,* 5th edition. Oxford: Blackwell Scientific Publications, 1992: 1699–746.
4. Jowett S, Ryan T. Skin disease and handicap: an analysis of the impact of skin conditions. *Social Science and Medicine* 1985; **20**: 425–9.
5. Layton AM, Stainforth JM, Cunliffe WJ. Ten years' experience of oral isotretinoin for the treatment of acne vulgaris. *Journal of Dermatological Treatment* 1993; **4** (Suppl 2): S2–S5.
6. Cunliffe WJ, Gray JA, Macdonald-Hull S *et al.* Cost of effectiveness of isotretinoin. *Journal of Dermatological Treatment* 1991; **1**: 285–8.
7. Molloy HF, Lamont-Gregory E, Idzikowski C, Ryan TJ. Overheating in bed as an important factor in many common dermatoses. *International Journal of Dermatology* 1993; **32**: 668–72.
8. Baran R, Dawber RPR (eds). *Diseases of the Nails and Their Management,* 2nd edition. Oxford: Blackwell Scientific Publications, 1994.
9. Brody S. The concepts of attachment and bonding. *Journal of the American Psychoanalytic Association* 1981; **29**: 815–29.
10. Ginsburg IH, Prystowsky JH, Kornfeld DS, Wolland H. Role of emotional factors in adults with atopic dermatitis. *International Journal of Dermatology* 1993; **32**: 656–60.
11. Salek MS, Finlay AY, Luscombe DK *et al.* Cyclosporin greatly improves the quality of life of adults with severe atopic dermatitis. A randomised, double-blind, placebo-controlled trial. *British Journal of Dermatology* 1993; **129**: 422–30.
12. Herd RM. Atopic eczema in the community: morbidity and cost. *British Journal of Dermatology (Abstract)* 1994; **131**: 909.
13. Ginsburg IH, Link BG. Pyschosocial consequences of rejection and stigma feelings in psoriasis patients. *International Journal of Dermatology* 1993; **32**: 587–91.
14. Camp RDR. Psoriasis. In: Champion RH, Burton JL, Ebling FJG (eds) *Rook, Wilkinson & Ebling Textbook of Dermatology,* 5th edition. Oxford: Blackwell Scientific Publications, 1992: 1391–457.
15. Goldstein N (ed). Tattoos. Special articles from *Journal of Dermatologic Surgery and Oncology* 1979; **4**(11): 847–916.

PART FOUR

Psychological aspects of adolescence

11 | Suicide and attempted suicide in young people

Keith Hawton
Consultant Psychiatrist and Senior Clinical Lecturer,
University Department of Psychiatry, Warneford Hospital, Oxford

Suicidal behaviour increasingly appears to be a feature of the young. Thus suicide rates in many countries have risen in young people, while in some they have fallen in older people. Rates of attempted suicide are usually highest in people in their teenage years and twenties. Suicidal behaviour is now one of the major health problems of young people. The Health of the Nation mental health targets have rightly focused on suicide. Thus one target is a 15% overall reduction in suicide rates by the year 2000, with a particular emphasis on reversing the recent dramatic rise in young male suicides.

There are many current issues in relation to suicide and attempted suicide in young people. Those considered here, focusing on people under the age of 25 years, include: recent changes in suicide rates, especially in the United Kingdom, and possible reasons for these; international differences in attempted suicide; issues concerning treatment of young suicide attempters, and current knowledge and research needs regarding their psychological characteristics; the important link between attempted suicide and subsequent suicide in the young; and, finally, possible strategies for prevention.

Trends in suicide in the young

Major changes in the patterns of suicide have occurred in recent years in several European countries and also in North America. The main trend has been an increase in suicide rates in young males. A marked change occurred in the USA during the 1960s and 1970s. Thus, between 1960 and 1981, suicide rates in American males aged 15–24 years more than doubled. Rates in females in the same age group also increased but to a lesser extent. Increased rates of suicide in young males have also been reported from several European countries, including especially Portugal,

Spain and Greece.[1] This phenomenon has also occurred in Australia, New Zealand and Japan.

This pattern has been particularly marked in the UK in the past 15–20 years. Between 1980 and 1992 the suicide rate for 15–24 year old males in England and Wales increased by more than 80%. The rate for deaths from undetermined cause, the majority of which are known to be suicides, increased even more—by 100%. Combining both rates for suicide and deaths from undetermined cause ('open verdict') revealed an overall rise of 86.3%. In contrast, the combined rates of suicide and undetermined deaths in 15–24 year old females changed very little over this time period (–5.5%). In 1992 there were 187 suicides and open verdicts in 15–19 year olds (146 males and 41 females) and 583 in 20–24 year olds (478 males and 105 females). Suicide is now the second most common reason (after accidents) for death in young males. However, suicide is rare under 15 years of age.

An important question is to what extent these changes may represent a cohort or period effect. If the former, then suicide rates in older age groups are likely to rise in future as the present generation of young people ages. It is of some comfort that in the USA, where the increase in rates for young males occurred earlier than in the UK, this has not been found.

Possible reasons for the recent changes in suicide rates in young people

Several possible explanations for the changing pattern of suicide in the young, especially the increase in male suicides, have been suggested[2] but at present there is no certainty about any of them (Table 1). When evaluating the explanations that have been suggested it is important to bear in mind the very different changes in suicide rates in the two sexes. Thus, to be valid, explanatory factors must either have occurred to different extents in the two sexes or have had very marked differential effects on males and females.

Unemployment

It has long been recognised that there are fairly strong statistical associations between rates of unemployment and rates of both suicide and attempted suicide.[1,3–6] However, the nature of this association is unclear. Thus, while it seems unlikely that unemployment itself more than occasionally directly leads to suicidal behaviour, there may be an indirect causal link, perhaps via, for example,

Table 1. Possible reasons for increasing rates of suicide in young males

1. Increasing unemployment
2. Increasing alcohol and drug abuse
3. Increased availability of methods for suicide
4. AIDS
5. Marital breakdown
6. Media influences
7. Social changes

poverty, social deprivation, domestic difficulties and hopelessness. On the other hand, the statistical association may be explained by people at risk for suicidal behaviour, especially those with chronic mental illness, being more likely to be unemployed. From the evidence available to date it seems likely that both types of explanation for the statistical association are relevant although the relative contribution of each remains unclear.

There are, however, difficulties in attributing the increase in suicide in young males to unemployment, at least in the UK. First, while suicide rates rose steadily during the 1980s and early 1990s, the unemployment rate declined in the later 1980s. Secondly, unemployment rates have also risen in females. One can argue with some justification, however, that the impact of unemployment on males may be somewhat different from that for females, particularly in terms of its greater implication for the self-esteem and social standing of males and its effects on their families and domestic circumstances. Female self-esteem may be less dependent on employment status and more related to other factors, such as personal relationships.

Alcohol and drug abuse

It is well recognised that suicide risk is strongly associated with both alcohol[7] and drug abuse.[8] Furthermore, rates of both types of abuse have risen in young people, at least in the UK. However, the increase in substance abuse has occurred in both sexes. It is possible that substance abuse may be an increasing factor in young suicides but differentially affect the two sexes because of its interaction with other factors (eg differences between the two sexes in ability to seek help for emotional problems).

A major psychological autopsy study of young suicides in New York has demonstrated the importance of substance abuse in suicides there, especially in males (Shaffer, personal communication). While depression was also common, interestingly this often developed after the onset of substance abuse rather than being the cause of it. A history of conduct disorder often preceded the substance abuse.

Increased availability of methods for suicide

It is also well known that availability of methods for committing suicide affects suicide rates, the best example being the large decline in suicides in the UK that paralleled the introduction of non-toxic North Sea gas during the 1960s.[9] Nowadays, car exhaust poisoning is one of the two most frequent methods used for suicide by young men in the UK. Could the increased number of young car owners, especially males, plus the publicity about such deaths, be a partial explanation for the increased number of suicide deaths?

Hanging is another common method in the young. This has increased in frequency in both sexes. There are a significant number of deaths each year because of paracetamol self-poisoning, an overdose of paracetamol carrying a significant risk of liver damage. In this country paracetamol is readily available.

AIDS

Suicide rates are greatly elevated in people with AIDS[10] (although some of the increased risk may be explained by other factors, especially drug abuse). However, AIDS cannot have contributed greatly to the increase in male suicide rates because, first, the increase in rates began well before AIDS was recognised in 1984, and, secondly, the number of AIDS-related suicides would have been far less than the actual increase in the number of male suicides that has recently occurred.[11] If the number of AIDS cases increases in future, however, this factor may increasingly influence suicide rates, although perhaps more in men in their thirties and forties rather than in the very young.

Media influences

There is reasonable evidence that media portrayal of suicide can influence suicide in other people, especially in the young. The best example is where a major increase in railway suicides occurred in Germany following the double showing of a serial on TV in which a 19 year old boy committed suicide on a railway.[12] This increase was not accompanied by a fall in use of other methods for suicide. On the other hand, little or no evidence has been found in this country of an influence of media portrayal of self-poisoning on rates of deliberate self-poisoning.[13] Nevertheless, such positive evidence as does exist makes one concerned about the potential effects on the suicide potential of vulnerable young people of dramatic reporting of actual suicides or media portrayal of fictional suicides.

Marital breakdown

This is relevant to risk of suicidal behaviour in the young in two major ways. First, there are the possible long-term effects of parental marital breakdown on children. Thus the rapid rise in rates of marital breakdown and divorce in the 1960s and 1970s may have increased the vulnerability of today's young people to experience emotional difficulties and hence suicidal behaviour.[14,15]

Secondly, the increased rate of breakdown of relationships in young people today may have contributed to their increased risk of suicide. This will of course be more relevant to people in their twenties than to teenagers. Since broken relationships occur with equal frequency in males and females, how might one explain the fact that rates of suicide in young males are increasing while those in females remain relatively stable?

A possible explanation is that the considerable social changes of the last two decades, particularly the 'liberation of females', have differentially affected the relative vulnerability of males and females to the effects of broken relationships. Nowadays, for example, it is far easier for women to live independently than was the case in, say, the 1960s. Also, females are generally more able to seek and find support from other females when facing emotional difficulties, such as following a broken relationship, whereas many males find it difficult both to admit to emotional difficulties and to seek help from peers or helping agencies.

My personal belief is that the most likely explanation for the increase in suicide rates in young men lies in social changes, as noted above, which have differentially affected the relative vulnerability of males and females to emotional difficulties, particularly in response to other stress factors such as unemployment and broken relationships, with substance abuse and difficulty in help-seeking being additional contributory factors. There is, however, a pressing need for more research to unravel the explanatory factors and hence to allow preventive strategies to be developed on the basis of sound knowledge. This highlights the need in this country for psychological autopsy studies of young suicides as well as sophisticated epidemiological investigations.

While several such studies have been conducted in other countries[16] these are only just beginning in the UK, including one by our research group. One clear finding that has already emerged and which is clearly relevant to possible preventive approaches is that relatively few young suicides, unlike older suicides, have been in contact with their general practitioners during the weeks preceding their deaths.[17] Thus focusing preventive efforts on primary care might have only limited potential.

Attempted suicide ('deliberate self-harm')

Attempted suicide became increasingly common during the late 1960s and early 1970s, particularly in young females. The highest rates of all ages are found in 15–19 year old females. Whereas the rates appeared to have declined somewhat in the early 1980s they have risen again since. In contrast to suicide, rates of attempted suicide are lower in males than females. It has been calculated that there are 18–19,000 suicide attempts by teenagers in the UK per year which result in hospital referral.[18] This is the most common reason for acute medical admission of young people.

The most common problems of young suicide attempters are difficulties in interpersonal relationships with partners or relatives, unemployment and employment difficulties (especially males), substance abuse and eating disorders. While many young suicide attempters have psychiatric (especially depressive) symptoms at the time of their acts, relatively few have persistent psychiatric disorders. There is a particular association between attempted suicide and childhood and adolescent abuse, including sexual abuse.

Most suicide attempts are by self-poisoning, and lately poisoning with paracetamol and paracetamol-containing compounds has become very common. The risk of liver damage has already been noted. Many attempts in this age group are impulsive, the majority of overdoses being taken with very little forethought.[19] The behaviour is often repeated, with at least 10% repeating their attempts within a year.[18]

In a European context we now know from the current WHO:EURO parasuicide study that rates of deliberate self-harm are especially common in young people, particularly females, in the UK.[20,21] Indeed it seems that the size of this problem in teenagers in the UK is greater than in almost any other country in

Europe. It is apparent that deliberate self-harm is also quite common in this country in adolescents between 12 and 15 years of age.

Of considerable interest are the very different rates of attempted suicide found in the UK compared with Holland, particularly since the rates of completed suicide in these two countries are fairly similar. The overall rates of attempted suicide in Oxford, for example, are some four times greater than in Leiden, with the difference in the young being even more marked.[21,22] Since 1989 a collaborative project has been conducted regarding attempted suicide in Oxford and Utrecht, based on data obtained through the attempted suicide monitoring systems in the two centres. A similar difference in the pattern of attempted suicide has been found, with relatively large numbers of young suicide attempters (especially adolescent females) in Oxford (which is reasonably representative of the situation regarding attempted suicide generally in the UK) and far fewer in Utrecht.[23]

Why should there be such differences? One possibility is that fewer Dutch young people have the sort of problems known to be associated with attempted suicide. Might family structures be closer and/or substance abuse problems less common in Dutch adolescents than in their counterparts in the UK? Or might attitudes to suicidal behaviour differ between young people in the two countries such that thresholds to non-fatal suicidal behaviour are lower in the young in the UK? Sociological investigations are required to answer these questions. However, one clue that the thresholds to suicidal behaviour might differ between the young in the two countries was the finding that the mean number of problems recorded per attempter was greater in Utrecht, although only in males. Also, psychiatric and personality disorders were more common in the Dutch attempters. Thus more stress or psychopathology may be required before the young in Holland are likely to resort to acts of deliberate self-harm.

Such comparative studies can be a fruitful way of investigating the causes of suicidal behaviour in different countries. Their results may have important implications in terms of possible preventive strategies. For example, findings that indicate different attitudes to suicidal behaviour may highlight the importance of educational approaches to prevention.[24]

Treatment and psychological processes in young suicide attempters

In the light of the higher rates of attempted suicide in young attempters, especially adolescents, compared with older adults it is very surprising that there have been virtually no controlled studies of treatment in this group. One exception was a study by Deykin *et al*[25] in Boston in the USA, which demonstrated that the ready availability of emergency help at a hospital for adolescents who had previously made attempts resulted in greater use of such a service compared with the frequency of help-seeking by other young attempters not provided with this special service. However, the experimental service did not result in any reduction in the frequency of repetition of attempts.

Since family relationship difficulties are extremely common in adolescent attempters[26] one might expect that family therapy might be the most productive way of helping youngsters following attempts. This approach appears, however, to be severely limited in effectiveness in many cases because of the high rate with which it is rejected by parents, as reflected by high levels of non-attendance at treatment sessions.[27] Further research on a family approach to treatment of adolescent suicide attempters is under way.

It is generally agreed that brief psychological treatment is appropriate for many attempters, including the young.[28] If such treatment is to be effective it needs to be based on a firm understanding of the psychological characteristics of young attempters. Considerable advances have been made in unravelling the psychological characteristics common to many adult attempters. Thus deficient problem-solving and abnormalities of autobiographical memory (reflecting overgeneralised memories of behaviours and experiences which influence mood) seem to distinguish many attempters from controls.[29] Far less is known, however, about the psychological characteristics of very young attempters, except that deficiencies in problem-solving skills have been demonstrated shortly after attempts.[30] We are currently investigating whether such deficits are state or trait characteristics. In other words, are they only found when the individual is in crisis or do they persist? In one study of adult attempters, contrary to what one might expect, deficits in problem-solving skills appeared to be state rather than trait characteristics. A similar finding emerged in a study of cognitive rigidity in suicide attempters.[31] This is clearly relevant to the development of effective aftercare programmes since addressing state characteristics is likely to involve somewhat different strategies from treatment focused on trait features. The findings from studies of psychological characteristics of young attempters should be used to enrich treatment programmes. These then need to be evaluated in randomised controlled trials.

Suicide following attempted suicide in young people

Follow-up studies of adolescent suicide attempters from Scandinavia[32] and the UK[33,34] have shown that there is a significant risk of subsequent completed suicide. Until recently little was known about the specific risk factors for completed suicide in young attempters, except that the risk is particularly high in males in their late teenage years. A recently completed study of suicide following attempted suicide in young people in Edinburgh aged 15–24 years at the time of their attempts has shown that a further key factor is substance (alcohol and/or drug) abuse.[35] Another was previous inpatient care but in many cases this may have reflected admission because of substance abuse. These factors were predictors in both the short term (less than one year) and longer term after attempted suicide.

Prevention of suicidal behaviour in young people

Clearly a multifactorial approach to prevention needs to be taken. As already noted, we badly need further information about the characteristics of young suicides. This is necessary for planning comprehensive preventive strategies.

The following are some possible strategies for preventing suicidal behaviour in young people.

Educational programmes in schools

Such programmes could focus on the pupils and staff. For pupils, programmes in life skills are probably the most desirable approach. Evidence from the USA suggests that these programmes should not focus specifically on suicide.[24] In addition teachers could be taught to recognise the signs of children with major psychological problems, including substance abuse, and risk factors for suicide.

Control/modification of methods used for suicidal behaviour

The introduction of efficient catalytic converters should have an impact on car exhaust suicides. However, since young suicides rarely involve new cars the impact of this approach may be long delayed. Changing the physical structure of exhaust outlets to prevent the insertion of a tube would be another and relatively simple measure. Prevention of paracetamol self-poisoning might best be achieved through reducing the number of tablets/capsules available per container.[36]

Efforts to reduce substance abuse

In view of the clear associations between substance abuse and both attempted suicide and suicide this needs to be a major focus in prevention efforts. First, further efforts should be directed towards the prevention of both alcohol and drug abuse in young people, through, for example, educational measures and (perhaps) taxation strategies with regard to alcohol costs. Secondly, assessment of young suicide attempters should always include careful screening for alcohol and substance abuse. Thirdly, and most pertinently, there is clearly a need for very close links between substance abuse services and general hospital services for young suicide attempters in order that those who are identified as having substance abuse problems can receive specialised treatment for this problem.

More responsible media reporting of suicide

In view of the evidence that suicides in young people may be facilitated by the media, especially in dramatic reports or dramas, it is desirable that the media be made fully aware of this and attempts made to make media presentation more responsible. It could be helpful if the actual method of suicide were not mentioned when reporting suicides in newspapers or on television. All dramas or other programmes about suicide on radio or television should be followed by adverts for helplines. Expert advice should always be sought in the planning of such programmes.

General hospital services for suicide attempters

These vary greatly in quality. They should be brought up to a high standard, with particular care about the services available for young attempters. For example, there should be very close links between hospital services for suicide attempters and those for substance abusers. The new Royal College of Psychiatrists consensus guidelines on the general hospital management of deliberate self-harm[37] should assist purchasers and providers in the development of good quality services.

Local working groups on suicide prevention

All districts/regions should establish working groups to investigate methods of suicide prevention locally. This should include a focus on suicidal behaviour in young people. Such groups should include representatives from psychiatry, general practice, public health, social services, education, the church and voluntary agencies.

Others

It is extremely important that psychiatric services for young people are generally of a high standard. Further potential means of prevention include provision of hot-lines and walk-in services and the extension of the role of voluntary agencies. Clearly several factors that are associated with suicide are the result of major social changes and policies. Such factors (eg unemployment and increasing rates of substance abuse in the young) must be highlighted forcibly to those able to influence relevant policies in this country.

Conclusions

Suicide and attempted suicide are major problems in young people and deserve our most serious attention. The dramatic recent increase in suicide in young males warrants very close study in order that methods of prevention might be identified. It has become apparent that not only is attempted suicide ('deliberate self-harm') common in young people but the situation in the UK in this regard might be as bad as anywhere in Europe. Again methods of prevention need to be sought, with perhaps educational strategies offering the most fruitful approach for primary prevention. In addition, general hospital services for young people who are referred following deliberate self-harm must be of a high standard.

Appendix: Advice to young people on what to do if a friend appears to be suicidal

If a close acquaintance seems to be distressed it is always useful to try and get them to discuss how they are feeling. Should the friend give any indication of thinking that he or she would be better off dead or is any way threatening suicide, it is important to act promptly. First, one should try to encourage the person to talk further about their feelings and then encourage them to seek help from someone, eg teacher, doctor, voluntary agency. While it is important, whenever possible, to respect confidentiality concerning personal matters that are revealed by friends, mention of suicide is a situation which usually presents an exception to this rule. One should discuss one's concerns with someone else, preferably an adult. While this may be seen as deceitful and not showing respect to the friend, it may be an important step in preventing that friend's suicide. One of the most important messages in suicide prevention is that it is not true that people who talk about suicide never do it, just the reverse.

Recommended reading

Hawton K. *Suicide and Attempted Suicide in Children and Adolescents.* Newbury Park, California: Sage, 1986.
Hill K. *The Long Sleep: Young People and Suicide.* London: Virago, 1995.

References

1. Pritchard C. Is there a link between suicide in young men and unemployment? *British Journal of Psychiatry* 1992; **160**: 750–6.
2. Hawton K. By their own young hand. *British Medical Journal* 1992; **304**: 1000.
3. Platt S. Unemployment and suicidal behaviour—a review of the literature. *Social Science and Medicine* 1984; **19**: 93–115.
4. Platt S, Kreitman N. Trends in parasuicide and unemployment among men in Edinburgh. *British Medical Journal* 1984; **289**: 1029–32.
5. Hawton K, Rose N. Unemployment and attempted suicide among men in Oxford. *Health Trends* 1986; **18**: 29–32.
6. Hawton K, Fagg J, Simkin S. Female unemployment and attempted suicide. *British Journal of Psychiatry* 1988; **152**: 632–7.
7. Murphy GE. *Suicides in Alcoholism.* New York: Oxford University Press, 1992.
8. Fowler RC, Rich CL, Young D. San Diego suicide study. II: Substance abuse in young cases. *Archives of General Psychiatry* 1986; **43**: 962–5.
9. Kreitman N. The coal gas story: UK suicide rates 1960–71. *British Journal of Preventative and Social Medicine* 1976; **30**: 86–93.
10. Marzuk P *et al.* Increased risk of suicide in persons with AIDS. *Journal of the American Medical Association* 1988; **259**: 1333–7.
11. Buehler J, Devine O, Berkelman R, Chevarley F. Impact of human immunodeficiency virus epidemic on mortality trends in young men, United States. *American Journal of Public Health* 1990; **80**: 1080–6.
12. Schmidtke A, Häfner H. The Werther effect after television films: new evidence for an old hypothesis. *Psychological Medicine* 1988; **18**: 665–76.
13. Platt S. The aftermath of Angie's overdose: is soap (opera) damaging to your health? *British Medical Journal* 1987; **294**: 954–7.
14. Dorpat TL, Jackson JK, Ripley HS. Broken homes and attempted suicide. *Archives of General Psychiatry* 1965; **12**: 213–6.
15. Bulusu L, Alderson M. Suicides 1950–1982. *Population Trends* 1984; **35**: 11–17.
16. Martunnen MJ, Aro HM, Lönnqvist JK. Adolescence and suicide: a review of psychological autopsy studies. *European Child and Adolescent Psychiatry* 1993; **2**: 10–18.
17. Vassilas CA, Morgan HG. General practitioners' contacts with victims of suicide. *British Medical Journal* 1993; **307**: 300–1.

18. Hawton K, Fagg J. Deliberate self-poisoning and self-injury in adolescents: a study of characteristics and trends in Oxford, 1976–89. *British Journal of Psychiatry* 1992; **161**: 816–23.

19. Hawton K. *Suicide and Attempted Suicide Among Children and Adolescents.* Newbury Park, CA: Sage Publications Inc, 1986.

20. Schmidtke A, Bille-Brahe U, DeLeo D, Kerkhof A *et al.* Rates and trends of attempted suicide in Europe 1989–1992. In: Kerkhof AJFM, Schmidtke A, Bille-Brahe U, DeLeo D, Lönnqvist J (eds) *Attempted Suicide in Europe: Findings from the Multicentre Study on Parasuicide by the WHO Regional Office for Europe.* Leiden University: DSWO Press, 1994.

21. Hawton K, Fagg J, Simkin S, Mills J. The epidemiology of attempted suicide in the Oxford area, England, 1989–1992. In: Kerkhof AJFM, Schmidtke A, Bille-Brahe U, DeLeo D, Lönnqvist J (eds). *Attempted Suicide in Europe.* Leiden: DSWO Press, Leiden University, 1994.

22. Platt S *et al.* Parasuicide in Europe: the WHO/EURO multicentre study on parasuicide. I. Introduction and preliminary analysis for 1989. *Acta Psychiatrica Scandinavica* 1992; **85**: 97–104.

23. Grootenhuis M, Hawton K, van Rooijen L, Fagg J. Attempted suicide in Oxford and Utrecht. *British Journal of Psychiatry* 1994; **165**: 73–8.

24. Shaffer D. Implications for education: prevention of youth suicide. In: Jenkins R, Griffiths S, Wylie I, Hawton K, Morgan G, Tylee A (eds). *The Prevention of Suicide.* London: HMSO, 1994: 163–73.

25. Deykin EY, Chung-Chen Hsieh, Joshi N. Adolescent suicidal and self-destructive behaviour: results of an intervention study. *Journal of Adolescent Health Care* 1986; **7**: 88–95.

26. Hawton K, O'Grady J, Osborn M, Cole D. Adolescents who take overdoses: their characteristics, problems and contacts with helping agencies. *British Journal of Psychiatry* 1982; **140**: 118–23.

27. Taylor EA, Stansfield SA. Children who poison themselves. II. Prediction of attendance for treatment. *British Journal of Psychiatry* 1984; **145**: 132–5.

28. Hawton K, Catalan J. *Attempted Suicide: A Practical Guide to its Nature and Management.* Oxford: Oxford University Press, 1987.

29. MacLeod AK, Williams JMG, Linehan MM. New developments in the understanding and treatment of suicidal behaviour. *Behavioural Psychotherapy* 1992; **20**: 193–218.

30. Rotheram-Borus MJ, Trautman PD, Dopkins SC, Shrout PE. Cognitive style and pleasant activities among female adolescent suicide attempters. *Journal of Consulting and Clinical Psychology* 1990; **58**: 554–61.

31. Schmidtke A, Schaller S. Covariation of cognitive styles and mood factors during crises. In: Crepet P, Ferrari G, Platt S, Bellini M (eds). *Suicidal Behaviour in Europe: Recent Research Findings.* Rome: John Libbey CIC, 1992.

32. Otto U. Suicidal acts by children and adolescents: a follow-up study. *Acta Psychiatrica Scandinavica* 1972; Supplement 233: pp 7–123.

33. Goldacre M, Hawton K. Repetition of self-poisoning and subsequent death in adolescents who take overdoses. *British Journal of Psychiatry* 1985; **146**: 395–8.

34. Sellar C, Hawton K, Goldacre MJ. Self-poisoning in adolescents:

hospital admissions and deaths in the Oxford Region 1980–85. *British Journal of Psychiatry* 1990; **156**: 866–70.

35. Hawton K, Platt S, Fagg J, Hawkins M. Suicide following parasuicide in young people. *British Journal of Psychiatry* 1993; **152**: 359–66.

36. Hawton K, Ware C, Mistry H, Hewitt J, Kingsbury S, Roberts D, Weitzel H. Paracetamol self-poisoning: characteristics, prevention and harm reduction. *British Journal of Psychiatry* (in press).

37. Royal College of Psychiatrists. *The General Hospital Management of Adult Deliberate Self-harm.* Council Report CR32. London: Royal College of Psychiatrists, 1994.

12 | Young people and illegal drugs

Philip Robson
Consultant Psychiatrist, Chilton Clinic,
Warneford Hospital, Oxford

Recent reports from the University of Exeter[1] indicate that almost a third of 15 year olds have experimented with illegal drugs, and studies in older teenagers and university undergraduates (Table 1) show clearly the startling prevalence of illicit drug use. Such surveys are of dubious reliability, but the consistency of the figures in different parts of the country and the anecdotal reports of teachers and doctors suggest that they reflect a worrying reality. The results are all the more striking for being based upon samples of

Table 1. Ever used street drugs (percentages)

	School students		Undergraduates
	Oxford* (*n* = 183) Mean age 17y	Manchester† (*n* = 776) Mean age 16y	Oxford‡ (*n* = 318)
Cannabis	48	41	57
Amphetamine	24	16	12
LSD	20	25	17
Solvents	12	12	9
MDMA (Ecstasy)	10	7	10
Tranquillisers	6	—	4
Cocaine	6	4	6
Heroin	(2)	2	(1)

Figures in brackets—individuals rather than percentages.
* Robson PJ (1994); unpublished observations.
† University of Manchester. Alcohol and drug use among North West youth. October 8 1993. Cited in *Druglink* November/December 1993, page 5.
‡ Sell LA, Robson PJ (1994); unpublished observations.

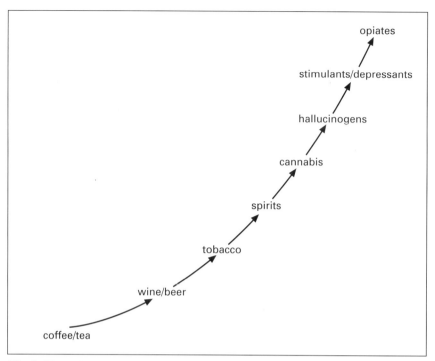

Fig 1. *Typical escalation of drug use*

young people progressing through secondary and tertiary education, rather than marginal groups of deviant teenagers.

Detailed analysis as to why people choose to experiment with recreational drugs is beyond the scope of this chapter, and has been summarised elsewhere.[2] Reasons include a search for pleasure or excitement, a desire to assert independence or gain status, to conform with the behaviour and attitudes of peers or to rebel against parental or other authority figures, to reinforce an internal or external image, or to self-medicate some unpleasant symptom such as anxiety or shyness. The escalation theory, which suggests that use of a drug such as cannabis might inexorably lead to, or in some way cause, a progression to 'hard' drugs, does not bear critical examination. Most people who try cannabis never move to any other drug. Although there is a discernible sequence for the majority of drug users (Fig 1), with a large majority of heroin addicts giving a history of earlier experimentation with cannabis, it is also true that almost all of them used alcohol and tobacco before that. If this is a causative sequence, one would have to track back to those substances proximal to cannabis, and conclude that the final addiction would never have occurred if only the person had not initially succumbed to the temptation to indulge in a cup of tea or coffee! The decision to use cannabis is significant, however, in one unfortunate way; it brings a large number of otherwise law-abiding citizens into contact with the criminal underworld.

Short-term risks

Experimentation carries a number of immediate risks. Any drug capable of producing intoxication may result in accidents on the roads or elsewhere. Street drugs do not enjoy high quality control in their manufacture and packaging. There is a huge variation in potency of street heroin, for example, with seized samples ranging in this author's experience from 10% to 80% diamorphine content. Since neither the street dealer nor his customer has any real idea of the purity of a particular batch, accidental overdose, carrying with it the life-threatening risk of respiratory depression, is always a possibility. Street amphetamine usually contains only around 10% amphetamine sulphate, leaving tremendous scope for toxic bulking agents or adulterants. The psychological consequences of a 'bad trip' following LSD or psilocybin-containing mushrooms can be devastating. Glue sniffing carries a steady mortality from asphyxia or cardiac arrhythmias. Idiosyncratic responses to MDMA (Ecstasy) which may prove fatal, though rare, are well documented.[3]

All street drugs are vulnerable to adulteration or impurity, including cannabis. This has been found on occasion to be impregnated with the dangerous hallucinogen phencyclidine to enhance its effect, or contaminated with pesticides, fungi or bacteria.[4] Some drugs are associated with cumulative tissue damage if used regularly. For example, the occasional use of cannabis is probably low in risk[5] but, as a consequence of the characteristic smoking technique of experienced cannabis consumers (deep inhalation and prolonged smoke retention to maximise absorption) and the higher content of irritant or carcinogenic particulates in the fumes in comparison with tobacco smoke, someone who smokes four joints daily faces comparable risks of lung damage to a person smoking twenty cigarettes a day.[6] Chronic inhalation of solvents can cause liver, kidney or neurological damage. Heavy stimulant use may result in psychotic illness or addiction. Those individuals who inject drugs risk many painful or life-threatening complications resulting from use of impure material, contaminated needles or syringes, or poor injection technique.

Nature of experimenters

What are the characteristics of people who experiment with drugs and the consequences for such experimenters in later life, and what influences the likelihood of a person progressing from experimentation to regular use? Cross-sectional, retrospective research cannot provide the answers to these fundamental questions because it is unable to separate cause from effect. Prospective, long-term studies are required, and these are few in number.

Shedler and Block[7] recruited a sample of 3 year old children and followed them up regularly until they were 18. The children were interviewed and given detailed, standardised questionnaires at 3, 4, 5, 11, 14 and 18 years. Quality of parenting was assessed when the children were 5. Out of an initial sample of 130, 101 young people were retained for the complete life of the cohort. At 18, 68% of the sample had tried cannabis, 39% had used it at least once a month, and 21% at least once a week; 37% had tried cocaine, 25% LSD, and 10% had experimented with amphetamine, barbiturates, benzodiazepines or inhalants.

The investigators separated the sample into three groups on the basis of their drug use: abstainers, who had never tried any illicit drug ($n = 29$); experimenters, defined as those who had used cannabis once a month or less, and no more than one other drug ($n = 36$); and frequent users, who had used cannabis once weekly or more, plus at least one other drug. Sixteen subjects could not be classified. It was found that the group with the healthiest psychological profile were the experimenters. In comparison, an abstainer was typically '. . . a relatively tense, overcontrolled, emotionally constricted individual who is somewhat socially isolated and lacking in interpersonal skills', while frequent users tended to be '. . . interpersonally alienated, emotionally withdrawn, and manifestly unhappy, [expressing] his or her maladjustment through undercontrolled, overtly antisocial behaviour'. Most importantly, these psychological differences were clearly discernible in the subjects' earliest years, long before exposure to drugs had occurred. Children who went on to use drugs frequently were likely to demonstrate the triad of 'interpersonal difficulties, poor impulse control, and emotional distress from an early age'. Again compared to the experimenters, the quality of parenting appeared lower in the other two groups. Two main conclusions were drawn: 'Problem drug use is a symptom, not a cause, of personal and social maladjustment', and 'the meaning of drug use can be understood only in the context of an individual's personality structure and developmental history'.

Long-term outcome

A number of observations can be made on the basis of other long-term, prospective research.[8-12] Modest, controlled consumption is much commoner than regular, heavy or compulsive use ('abuse'), and many young people seem able to use illicit drugs in the same socially appropriate way that most adults are able to use alcohol. Such transient or experimental use does not seem to be associated with measurable long term harm. In one study involving a 1 year observation period, cigarettes were associated with more disruption of health than alcohol, cannabis or hard drugs.[9] On the other hand, an early onset of legal or illegal recreational drug use, or significant escalation in the teenage years, are bad prognostic signs. Regular or heavy consumption of these drugs during adolescence has a strong association with later mental and physical problems, difficult family, social and sexual relationships, and disruption of education and employment. Problem drug use overlaps with many other undesirable behaviours such as delinquency, teenage pregnancy and school drop-out, and probably shares many causative antecedents.

These studies and others[13] suggest a number of factors which increase the chance of an experimenter progressing to heavier use or addiction. These include physiological attributes related to genetics and neurochemical balance; certain personality traits, mood states, and attitudes to self and the world in general; parental attitudes and behaviour, family structure and stability, and intra-family relationships; peer influences; the success or otherwise of the school in capturing and maintaining the child's interest and involvement; socioeconomic conditions; and availability and exposure to the drugs. Having stable and loving parents, a supportive family structure, a non-deviant peer group, clear goals and commitments all greatly reduce the probability of progression to problem drug use.

Prevention of drug misuse

Research into the effectiveness or otherwise of strategies aimed at preventing drug abuse have been extensively reviewed by a study group under the auspices of the American National Institute on Drug Abuse.[14]

Programmes should be guided by the knowledge that the average age of initiation into cigarette and cannabis use is between 12 and 13 years, and should have two distinct aims: to delay the onset of experimentation in 10 to 12 year olds, and minimise harm in those aged 13 and over, many of whom can be assumed to be experimenting already, or know people that have taken this step. There must be awareness that material intended for those who have had no exposure to drugs may be counterproductive if given to those who have. Provision of accurate, non-alarmist information will be an essential element of any programme, but is not in itself sufficient to bring about measurable behaviour change. Students must be involved in debate and discussion, and should be taught relevant social skills such as assertiveness, problem-solving, stress management, and how to resist social pressures. Confidence-boosting and ambition-raising are important, whilst scare-mongering or moralising can be actively counterproductive. The authors point out that initiation rates into drug use are remarkably constant across economic class groups, whilst abuse and dependence are vastly more prevalent amongst the poor and disenfranchised.[14]

Conclusions

Illegal drugs form an inescapable part of the environment in which young people grow up, and the majority of people in their twenties will have tried at least one. Covert drug use can cause or simulate physical illness, and simulate, modify or precipitate mental illness, and it is important that general practitioners and other doctors keep this in mind and take the necessary diagnostic steps.[15] Drug effects are unpredictable because they depend not just on pharmacology but also on the dose, the route of administration, the presence of adulterants or impurities, the mood, personality and expectations of the user, and the environment in which the drug is taken. Undeclared drug use should be suspected if there are reports of changing sleep patterns, unpredictable behaviour or mood swings, secretiveness or suspiciousness, changes in eating habits or weight, lethargy, restlessness or irritability, poor memory and concentration, or deteriorating school performance. Solvent abuse may be signalled by odd smells in the house, discarded plastic bags, cans, bottles or rags; spill marks or stains on clothes, especially sleeves; spots or ulcers round the nose and mouth; cracked lips, or chronic cough and runny nose. Teachers, parents, and others who might come into contact with young people in difficulties should be alert to the possibility that drugs (including alcohol) might be contributing.

The majority of illicit drug use among teenagers is experimental and short-term. Use of cigarettes and alcohol, and to a lesser extent cannabis, tends to be more protracted. Prospective research suggests that most people will not sustain measurable long-term harm from transient or short-term use, so adults should beware of causing more harm than good by over-reaction. Experimentation at an early age or escalation during the teenage years is associated with a greater likelihood of problems later. High frequency of cannabis use correlates with a greater probability of experimentation with other drugs. Regular or heavy use of cigarettes or illicit drugs in adolescence is clearly associated with a range of difficulties in adult life, but is more likely to be a symptom, rather than a cause, of personal and social maladjustment.[7] Prevention programmes based on information-giving alone do not result in measurable changes in behaviour.

References

1. Schools Health Education Unit. *Young people and illegal drugs 1989–1995: facts and predictions.* University of Exeter, 1994.
2. Robson PJ. Why use drugs? In: *Forbidden Drugs.* Oxford University Press, 1994: 3–12.
3. Henry JA. Toxicity and deaths from Ecstasy. *Lancet* 1992; **340**: 384–7.
4. James RT. Cannabis and health. *Annual Review of Medicine* 1983; **34**: 247–58.
5. Wootton Committee. *Cannabis: Report by the Advisory Committee on Drug Dependence.* London: HMSO, 1968.
6. Tashkin DP. Pulmonary complications of smoked substance abuse. *Western Journal of Medicine* 1990; **152**: 525–30.
7. Shedler J, Block J. Adolescent drug use and psychological health: a longitudinal inquiry. *American Psychologist* 1990; **45**: 612–30.
8. Kandel DB, Davies M, Karus D, Yamaguchi K. The consequences in young adulthood of adolescent drug involvement. *Archives of General Psychiatry* 1986; **43**: 746–55.
9. Newcomb MD, Bentler PM. The impact of late adolescent substance use on young adult health status and utilization of health services: a structural equation model over four years. *Social Science and Medicine* 1987; **24**: 71–82.
10. Newcomb MD, Bentler PM. Impact of adolescent drug use and social support on problems of young adults: a longitudinal study. *Journal of Abnormal Psychology* 1988; **97**: 64–75.
11. Hawkins JD, Catalano RF, Miller JY. Risk and protective factors for alcohol and other drug problems in adolescence and early adulthood: implications for substance abuse prevention. *Psychological Bulletin* 1992; **112**: 64–105.
12. Newcomb MD, Scheier LM, Bentler PM. Effect of adolescent drug use on adult mental health: a prospective study of a community sample. *Experimental and Clinical Psychopharmacology* 1993; **1**: 215–41.
13. Robson PJ. The nature of addiction. In: *Forbidden Drugs.* Oxford University Press, 1994: 153–72.

14. Gerstein DR, Green LW. *Preventing Drug Abuse: What Do We Know?* Washington DC: National Academy Press, 1993.
15. Robson PJ. Illegal drug use: a practical guide for general practitioners. *Primary Care Psychiatry* Vol 1 No 4 Dec 1995: 213–25.

PART FIVE

Rights to health care

13 | Do children's and young people's rights to health care in the UK ensure their best interests?*

Zarrina Kurtz
Consultant in Public Health and Health Policy, London

Changing situation of children and parents since the lifetime of Dr Gavin Milroy (1805–86)

The premise for health care is that it is in people's best interests. As physicians, we can just about come to terms with the discomfort we feel—on the recent widespread public exposure through Alan Bennett's play[1] and now the film on the madness of George III—at the manifest and cruel failure of the King's physicians to act in his best interests. We can remind ourselves that we have learnt more about disease processes since that time and about the art of healing and would do better now. But the careful historical analysis of George III's illness and the responses of his doctors, upon which these dramas are based, raises many questions that are as relevant today about the capacity of health care professionals and the system to act in the patient's best interests.[2] Little heed was paid to the King's rights—and they were above all others in the land at the time. Now it has been suggested by Michael Freeman, editor of the *International Journal of Children's Rights* which has been published since 1993, that 'rights' may be the key concept in contemporary philosophy,[3] pointing out that there is nothing new in this. The idea that political morality and social choice are governed by consideration of the rights of the individual arose from the writings of Locke and Kant and in the constitutions of the American and French revolutions. Rights have gained new prominence in health care both in the individual clinical situation and in service planning.

---

*This chapter is based on the Milroy Lecture delivered at the Royal College of Physicians on 3 May 1995 and previously published in *Journal of the Royal College of Physicians of London* 1995; **29**: 508–16.

Talking no longer of kings, what about children? There has been enormous growth in our knowledge and understanding about childhood and the experience of children. Three years ago, the United Kingdom signed up to the 1989 United Nations Convention on the Rights of the Child which places in international law, for the first time, a duty upon states to accord children rights on a par with adults. And it may be no coincidence that, at this time, the British Paediatric Association is seeking approval from the Privy Council to become a college independent of the Royal College of Physicians.*

Dr Gavin Milroy was married but had no children.[4] I have found no record as to whether no child was born to the couple or whether no children survived. Milroy died in 1886 at the age of 81. During the period of his lifetime, one child in five died within a year after birth and one in three before the end of their fifth year.[5] Milroy's life work was devoted to the control of communicable disease and to improving sanitary conditions and these were, at that time, the major causes of mortality in infants and children, and also of mothers dying. Even though maternal mortality was of the order of one for every 200 live births, ten times as many women of childbearing age died of other causes, most commonly pulmonary tuberculosis.[6] Many children, then, grew up without their mothers.

Over Milroy's lifetime, Dickens was campaigning for improvement in the living conditions and treatment of children and, although he showed little regard for what doctors could do, he was enormously influential in founding the Hospital for Sick Children in Great Ormond Street.[7] That the work of this great children's hospital can and still does attract very large sums of money may seem evidence that children's wellbeing is well supported in this country. However, the work on the streets, as it were, has never received anything like similar attention over the century and more since Dickens' time.

Control of communicable disease and improved hygiene are well understood concerns of public health and of the state, as is access to health care for children. Campaigns like that carried out by Dickens have spearheaded improvement in living conditions, and helped bring about smaller families, less overcrowding, better nutrition, and very great improvement in the health of children. This is most clearly shown by the huge drop in infant mortality rates and the increase in life expectancy from birth since those

---

*Approval has since been granted.

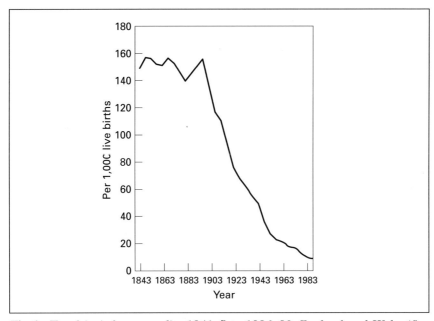

Fig 1. *Trend in infant mortality 1841–5 to 1986–90, England and Wales (five year averages).* Source: OPCS DH1/19 and DH2/17

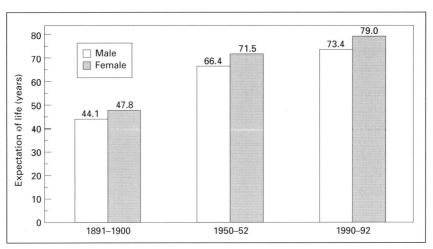

Fig 2. *Expectation of life at birth in England and Wales, 1891 to 1992.* Source: OPCS and Government Actuary's Department

times (Figs 1 and 2).[5,8] The classic account of the history of childhood by Philippe Ariès suggests that high rates of death in children led to a widespread feeling of indifference towards this fragile childhood.[9] But as it became less likely that children would die in infancy, ideas changed and there was a 'connection between progress in the concept of childhood and the progress of hygiene, between concern for the child and concern for his health'. The health and education of middle class children had become a prime concern of parents by the end of the eighteenth century. Ariès also argued that the concept of a long childhood was linked to the success of educational institutions in promoting the value of investing in education of the young. Childhood became in essence the period in which schooling took place. Because of their limited opportunities for schooling, the concept of a brief childhood lasted for much longer among the lower classes.

There are conflicting views of the general way in which children were regarded. The author of the catalogue to a recent exhibition at the Bibliothèque Nationale in Paris, about childhood in the Middle Ages, states that 'if there is truth in the statement that there was no place for children in the medieval world, it rests in the perception that children are to be found not in well defined and fenced-off areas such as nurseries, homes and schools, but everywhere in this society. We meet them and the evidence of their fortunes in almost every kind of record, from works of art and literature to manorial surveys and ecclesiastical legislation'.[10]

I suggest that we may be able to trace systematic differences in attitudes to children in different countries. And we can perhaps understand where the protective attitudes towards children were rooted in this country and also the treatment of children otherwise as mini-adults. Twenty years ago, the Court Committee spelled out the implications of the ways in which we view childhood for health care practice and services: 'In the last two or three generations we have come to realise their needs as being different from those of adults. At one time children were dressed in adult clothes scaled down to size, which seemed to reflect an attitude that they were in a sense retarded adults. Childhood was thought of as an inadequate and incomplete form of the adult state. By contrast we have become increasingly aware of childhood as a separate state, as a period of human experience in its own right. And more important still, we have come to realise the extent to which experience in childhood determines adult outcome.'[11]

That there is variation in the forms that families take is now well recognised but Lawrence Stone, in his history of the family in England, states that 'the only steady linear change [of the family] over the last four hundred years seems to have been a growing concern for children, although the actual treatment has oscillated cyclically between repression and permissiveness'.[12] It is in this climate that responsibility for children's interests has for the most part been assumed under ideas about what the family should or could do. Thus children are considered more or less as the property of their parents. This seems to lead to there being no need to account for children in their own right, either in terms of collecting information directly about their status or of targeting policy and action consistently towards their best interests. In addition, assumptions about parental responsibility for children mean that society takes the responsibility to interfere only in exceptional cases, when children are endangered.[13] The good of children depends upon paternalistic and benevolent attitudes of parents, of the state, and of professionals.

There is clearly a mutuality between parents and children, with parents as active and influential in the development of their children but also with their personal development influenced by having children. The distinction between adulthood and the more recent traditional characteristics of childhood is becoming less clear. Because adults now reckon to go on learning all their lives, being educated is certainly not uniquely a function of childhood. Adults will move more and more in and out of periods of work; therefore, not being in the job market or world of work will no longer be a defining characteristic of childhood either. Children in increasingly frequent situations look after or care for their parents or other adults and increasingly are not cared for by them. However, older members of families and of society dominate social policy. In Britain, a primary school child can now normally expect to live longer as a grandparent than as a parent only or as a child.[14] In addition, today's parents have become adults over a time during which enormous encouragement has been given to the idea that personal development and self-fulfilment should continue throughout life—tending to produce a cult of individualism which conflicts with the parenting role.

Children and young people have always been targeted by health care programmes, more in the spirit of charity or the interests of adult society than of entitlement by rights. Voluntary bodies and local education boards provided meals and milk at school when the introduction of compulsory schooling in Britain in the nineteenth century revealed the extent of malnutrition and physical defects for the first time. And in response to the finding that between 40 and 60% of men enlisting for the South African War were unfit for service, the state set up the school medical service in 1907 to carry out health inspections on all young people at school and later to ensure treatment. Maternity and child welfare services were established after the First World War. And responsibility for these local authority programmes was taken on by the NHS follow-ing the National Health Service Act of 1974. From the first NHS Act of 1946, seven rights have been restated recently in the 1991 Patient's Charter. These include that:

> every citizen has the right
> 1. to receive health care on the basis of clinical need, regardless of ability to pay; and
> 2. to be given a clear explanation of any treatment proposed, includ-ing any risks and any alternatives, before you decide whether you will agree to treatment.[15]

The NHS Patient's Charter rights are based on the Citizen's Char-ter.[16] A 'citizen' as applied to all public services, is a taxpayer and can vote. Children under the age of 18 cannot vote and therefore by definition in this country are not citizens in this sense. The Patient's Charter was developed as part of the recent fundamental reforms under the 1990 NHS and Community Care Act. During its implementation in the years following, it has become clear that children's interests have been largely regarded as covered by the 1989 Children Act.

The Children Act

The Children Act reinforced the underlying ethos of the Court Committee, embodying the view of the child as 'subject' as opposed to 'object'. The Act seeks primarily to support parents and takes 'as the fundamental task of parenthood, the duty to care for the child and to raise him to moral, physical and emotional health. The Act seeks to strike a balance between the need to recognise the child as an independent person and to ensure that his views are fully taken into account, and the risk of casting on him the burden of resolving problems caused by his parents or requiring him to choose between them'.[17] The Children Act makes radical changes in the law relating to children and their families, and states that in all matters of law 'the child's welfare shall be the court's paramount consideration'.

Children in need

New duties are placed upon local authorities to promote the upbring-ing of children in need. A child should be taken to be in need if:

(a) he is unlikely to achieve or maintain, or to have the opportun-ity of achieving or maintaining, a reasonable standard of health or development . . .

(b) his health or development is likely to be significantly impaired, or further impaired . . .

(c) he is disabled . . . Section 17(10)

'Development' means physical, intellectual, emotional, social or behavioural development; and 'health' means physical or mental health (Section 17(11)).

Rights to health care are only important to the extent that they have a bearing on rights to health. It often comes as a surprise when one has reviewed all that has been done and is in place for the promotion of health in children and young people that, in this country today, large numbers of children remain vulnerable. There may be fewer deaths among children and young people but the incidence and prevalence of chronic medical conditions such as asthma, diabetes, cerebral palsy and cystic fibrosis are rising, as are all types of disability.[8] Between 10 and 20% of children and young people show significant emotional and behavioural disorder at any one time and this proportion is on the increase.[18] In addition, there is a continuing and widening discrepancy between the health experience of children living in poor as compared to affluent socioeconomic conditions with clear indications that health care, among other services, is inadequate.[19] There is also good evidence that the number of children and young people in this country at serious risk of ill health because they are living in families with below half the average income is growing.[20,21] These indicators of conditions under which the risks to health of children are shown to be greatly increased tend to rely on relative measures but attempts have been made to describe the extent of need for a number of basic conditions for health by establishing a 'bottom-line' level below which health would be impaired.

Phillip Graham, recently appointed chairman of the National Children's Bureau, has defined the basic needs of children as those that are necessary for physical survival, for the avoidance of ill health and ignorance, and for preparation for an independent, autonomous role in adult society.[22] He has set out these basic needs as:

- an adequate diet,
- adequate housing,
- adequate income,
- a stable, continuous source of affection and care, together with protection from physical, emotional and sexual abuse,
- cognitive stimulation and adequate education,
- safe environment,
- access to preventive and curative health care.

This list is, by Professor Graham's own admission, somewhat arbitrary but could be defended. It can be demonstrated that in each of these areas, clear-cut failure to meet the need will result either in death, physical impairment, intellectual retardation, disturbed behaviour or emotions, or will subsequently lead to failure to lead an independent existence. Further, in each of these areas, the processes whereby failure to meet the need impairs physical or mental health are at least partially understood. To establish a standard for each of these basic needs below which there is an unacceptable degree of deprivation is more problematic. But we do know that significant numbers of children are living in conditions where their basic needs cannot be met.

Figure 3—published in *The Independent* on 25 November 1994—was taken as part of a project on child poverty in modern Britain. It comes with the following information:

> It is late afternoon when the children have returned from school for their largest meal of the day. The family live in a homeless families' hostel, with mother, father and six children in a two-room annex. The six children share three beds all in the same room. The children are

Fig 3. *Photograph taken as part of a project on child poverty in modern Britain.* © Craig Easton/The Independent: Reproduced with permission.

stigmatized at school for being so poor. Mother and father are both unemployed and rent is paid to the hostel by the Department of Social Security only because the father has no income. If he got a job, his pay would not cover the rent and he would have to look for somewhere else to live. But without a permanent address he has very little chance of getting work.

As a framework for ensuring equity and quality in health care, the Children Act has limitations. In law, services are to be available for disadvantaged children—an attempt to give an equitable share to those who suffer inequalities and an exercise in positive discrimination, in that those who are covered by the Act have a right to services while others may be by-passed. But the Children Act does not cover all children, and the criteria for categorisation as eligible for services—as a child in need—have been shown in the Annual Children Act Reports to vary widely between different authorities. And in a number of instances, services are not available for children who do meet the criteria.[23]

The Children Act must also be considered along with statute in other sectors which often acts counter to children's best interests in matters of health. For example, in order to meet imperatives arising from the 1993 Education Act, many education authorities are withdrawing resources such as educational psychologists and specialist teachers from multidisciplinary teams in health care settings such as child guidance clinics.[24] And for children with certain conditions, obtaining health care services may depend on obtaining a statement of special educational needs under the 1981 Education Act. Here again, different criteria apply to eligibility for a statement in different local authorities.[25] This situation has led to families who are eligible sometimes being inundated with services whereas, in reality, perhaps they can manage with much less or may need no services at all at a particular period. Parents have also sought the expensive, troublesome business of obtaining a statement if their child is 'eligible', even though they are well provided for, as an insurance for entitlement should they require help.[26]

Child protection

I now return to what has become the prime concern of the Children Act—child protection. Here, the extent of local discretion on the point at which intervention in the family is thought necessary is also very variable. There are no explicit national and accepted parenting standards which can reasonably be used to measure the success or otherwise of the Children Act in operation. A recent death through neglect of a baby in Islington revealed home-life conditions in which the children in the family had been living for 15 years. David Townsend, Director of Social Services for Croydon, writes that it was reported that the simplest kind of care was wholly absent: no clean clothes for the unwashed children, no hot water, no proper lavatory, few cooked meals and a lack of regular education. The house, which had been renovated and fully re-equipped before being wrecked, lacked warmth, light, bed-sheets, beds and toys. The Social Services department's only real action was to provide occasional financial hand-outs, and the family in which the baby died of neglect was described as 'smelly, dirty but happy'.[27]

This tolerance may be contrasted with the approach social ser-vices now take to adults under Community Care legislation. All departments are required to publish needs assessment criteria: these usually include basic elements such as appropriate accommo-dation, meals, personal hygiene and continence, domestic hygiene, safety for self and others, and maximised income. Some also include recreation and stimulation. In that framework it is clear what 'neglect' would be and what an adult has the right to expect.[27]

Links with health services are problematic under the Children Act because, as stated in Section 27 of the Act, a health authority must comply with the request for help from a local authority only provided that the request is compatible with its own statutory or other duties and does not unduly prejudice the discharge of its function. This implicitly recognises the likelihood of differing pri-orities between health and local authorities. A wide range of needs for health care are not included under the Children Act definition of a child in need and are also in danger of not being recognised in this frame of duties for local authorities.

In the NHS, a system of resource allocation and thereby of rationing has been introduced, also based on the concept of need. In the reformed NHS internal market arrangements, purchasing authorities place contracts with the providers of services based on assessment of the population's needs. Strictly speaking, in the assessment of health care needs, need is taken to mean the known ability to benefit from defined services.[28] Other important factors must be taken into account: epidemiological information which reflects what is known about the incidence and prevalence of disor-ders and risk factors in the population; information on the effec-tiveness of treatments, including cost-effectiveness; comparative assessments of performance, price and utilisation of existing ser-vices; and a 'corporate' view which takes account of the interests of local people, of general practitioners, providers and their clinical staff, and other local agencies including the voluntary sector. Needs assessment must also take account of priorities set by the Department of Health and other national, government and statutory bodies. It appears that all those in need will surely be identified and appropriate services made available through this comprehensive process but there is no unifying concept of need, even within the health service. This is increasingly recognised, as for example in this statement, made even in 1988, at the end of the introduction to the Royal College of Physicians report on the Medical Care of the Newborn in England and Wales:

> Finally . . . there is the question of whether we can better afford the economic cost of providing appropriate standards of care for ill newborn babies, or the moral cost of failing to do so . . .

Public health is now closely involved in setting priorities for health care provision, in purchasing and in specifying what should be purchased, based on assessment of needs. Public health, along with health care policy-makers, decision-takers, individual clinicians, and with society at large, must be concerned with the rights of children as of those of all members of the population because the influences on health now at the end of the twentieth century—although importantly including communicable disease, hygiene and nutrition as continuing concerns—are dominated by personal attitudes and behaviour—and I include the attitudes and behaviour of professionals and of politicians. The major hope for improving health lies in changing people's behaviour—as individuals and as groups. At an individual level, people may be persuaded to act in ways that increase their chances of staying healthy or of regaining health. In health care as a public service, there is increasing emphasis on what the patient or consumer, as an individual or collectively, wants, feels, thinks and knows. This is seen as central to delivering effective care and in deciding on priorities.

There has been increasing emphasis, now embodied in the Children Act, on the involvement of parents in decisions about children's health care. Parents generally provide practically all the care for their children's health, although occasionally they may be irresponsible in this respect. A number of studies have demonstrated how differently health professionals and parents (chiefly mothers) view their respective roles in parenting and in the health care of their children, and about the relative importance of particular health care problems or aspects of management.[29]

Parenting education is being developed apace, with the aim of better equipping parents to act in the best interests of their children and recognising that, if parenting and the role of Winnicott's ordinary 'good enough' mother were more highly valued, children would also fare much better.[30,31]

Nevertheless, individual case after case has now been documented of the grave consequences of different interpretations of the Children Act in relation to parenting roles and responsibilities. The following examples were given by a child and adolescent psychiatrist colleague.[32] He describes how the need to demonstrate that everything has been tried to maintain a child with his or her family may lead to such delay in placing a disturbed child in a foster family that his or her problems are worsened, making it then extremely difficult to place the child; he describes how paying attention to the rights of relatives may mean that a child is moved from pillar to post to be cared for or kept in a state of limbo, causing severe anxiety and behavioural disturbance; and how upholding the wishes to remain at home of a 10 year old boy who is out of his mother's control and extremely abusive to her may lead to complete disintegration of the parent–child relationship.

It has become clear that skills and a particular approach, with generous allocation of time, are required to ascertain children's wishes properly, especially those of very young children, and to tread the delicate line between listening to the child and listening to the parents. This aspect has so far been paid little attention in the UK, perhaps because it has been thought that the multidisciplinary approach to care would ensure that all contexts and considerations for the good of the whole child would be taken into account. However, we now have good evidence that decisions about individual case management and about common standards of practice and service protocols often are different according to the views of different members of a clinical team, of different professional groups and even of members of the same professional group. Personal values are found to have a profound effect on these decisions.[33] A great deal of attention has been paid in America, notably at the Yale Child Study Centre, to training multidisciplinary teams in working outside their individual professional interests but together, for the best interests of the child.[34] In Britain, this approach has for the most part been seen as perpetuating the power of professionals and, if not, of parents in deciding children's best interests. There is valid criticism about the difficulty of identifying the criteria that should be used to evaluate alternative options that are open to a decision-maker seeking (or purporting) to act in the child's best interest. In Mnookin's view 'the choice of criteria is inherently value-laden; all too often there is no consensus about what values should inform particular choices. The problems are not unique to children's policies, but are especially acute in this context because children themselves often cannot speak for their own interests'.[35]

That the child's wishes be taken into account in all matters of serious concern to him or her is written in the Children Act as one of a checklist of factors to which the court shall have particular regard as 'the ascertainable wishes and feelings of the child concerned (considered in the light of his age and understanding)'. In health care, this is one of the cardinal principles in the Department of Health's 1991 guidance on the *Welfare of Children and Young People in Hospital.*[36]

> Like all other patients, children have a right for their privacy to be respected and to be treated with tact and understanding. They have an equal right to information appropriate to their age, understanding and specific circumstances . . . Young people should be kept as fully informed as possible about their treatment so as to enable them to exercise their rights. Even where young children do not have the required understanding, they should be provided with as much information as possible and their wishes ascertained and taken into account.

Both the Act and the Department of Health guidance build on the pioneering work of the National Association for the Welfare of Children in Hospital (NAWCH), a parent-led organisation which was set up because of the distress experienced by parents and children when children were admitted into hospital to unfamiliar, often uncomfortable, surroundings and removed from their parents. The parents' views were greatly supported by a filmed record made by James Robertson of the largely unspoken messages of distress in a 5 year old in hospital. It is interesting to note how humane treatment of children has been introduced on the basis of evidence of the deleterious effects of neglect—and often depends on this evidence. A further example is that only in the last couple of years have infants undergoing surgery uniformly been properly anaesthetised. It was assumed that they did not feel pain or that, if they did, it did not matter. Only when post-surgery outcomes were shown in a scientific trial to be better in infants given complete anaesthesia was the extent of stress and pain suffered by babies who were incompletely anaesthetised appreciated.[37] Neonates having surgery cannot speak but, from work such as that of Priscilla Alderson on children's consent to surgery, we now have clear evidence that even very young children appreciate many of the issues that are important in their health care and can contribute helpful views on treatment and management.[38] The chief barrier to fully taking account of children's views and wishes in regard to health care is the presumption upon which so-called 'Gillick' competence is based. This is the evaluation of the ability of a child under the age of 16 to make his or her own medical decisions, according to age but considered in conjunction with the child's mental and emotional maturity, intelligence and comprehension—each of which requires fairly expert assessment to establish a level of competence.[39]

It is suggested that we will learn more if we turn around the starting point—in other words, we should presume that the child is competent unless he proves to be otherwise, not that he is not competent unless he shows himself to be competent. The key to children's rights is respect for their competence and acceptance that they can be as rational as adults. The 'non-competent child' who figures in the legal imagination is treated as arational rather than irrational. This leads to the recent uneasy swing between defining ages for the attainment of criminal responsibility.[40] But we must now build on the increasing evidence that children are capable of being moral agents; that they can voluntarily seek to promote the wellbeing or freedom of others.[41] It is also being shown now that even primary school children are interested in and capable of philosophical argument.[42]

In consideration of consent, competence is seen to depend almost entirely on the understanding of medical and legal information; professional, textbook knowledge is highly valued, personal experiential knowledge is discounted. Children are assumed to be ignorant, except in so far as they can recount medical information, whereas even decisions about major surgery involve both medical and personal knowledge.[38] There is an onus on professionals to take proper time and to develop their skills in giving information to patients. On the whole, they do not do this well, particularly with children and young people.[38]

The 'best interests' principle

The balance between professional, parental and the child's duties, responsibilities and rights is currently being redistributed and the boundaries between these and the child's best interests are still uncertain. There are differing considerations for the best interests of very young children, for progressively older children, for teenagers, and for young people which cannot be discussed in this article.

The case of 'B', the 10 year old girl with myeloid leukaemia, raises all the questions as to whose choice of best interests is acted upon. I should note that my account of this case is based entirely upon what I have read in the newspapers and the law reports.[43,44] B's father appealed to the High Court to overturn the district health authority's decision not to fund a further course of treatment for his daughter. B's clinicians had ostensibly not really grappled with the best interests issue except to decide against a further course of treatment because the chances of success were felt to be too low and the suffering caused by the treatment unacceptably great. In making their decision, they had consulted with other highly regarded specialists in the field. Professional opinion in this case cannot yet be comprehensively supported by rigorous scientific evidence as the condition is too rare for there to have been enough cases to study in a trial that could yield valid findings as to the outcomes of various approaches to management.

Costs were almost certainly present in the clinicians' thinking somewhere, including the costs in suffering to the child, the emotional costs to staff of putting a lot of effort into something that is almost certain to fail; perhaps the opportunity costs of their time *vis-à-vis* what could be spent on other patients; perhaps also the cost of a recorded outcome of the performance of their unit that would score low when monitored—a cynical view but one that must figure in the cost-effectiveness, performance management driven NHS. The health authority decision was expressed in this frame—according to clinical and, secondarily, to cost effectiveness. One measure of effectiveness—cure or remission—was given very much greater emphasis than the quality of life dimension. Measurement of quality of life requires the views of the person or people with the condition under question.[45]

In B's case, a doctor practising in the private sector was ready to carry out treatment if funds could be found. A practitioner in this situation earns more, the more he treats. Ostensibly, he like others practising outside the NHS is offering a service in line with what consumers want. But private hospitals where these treatments can be given frequently do not support comprehensive paediatric facilities with appropriately trained and experienced staff as recommended for the care of childhood leukaemia by the Clinical Standards Advisory Group,[46] nor are their service contracts likely to specify or to monitor quality standards for the care of children such as those laid down in the NAWCH Charter[47] and the Department of Health guidance.[36] Over 90% of those who phoned in to Nick Ross's radio programme at the time said that B should be offered treatment on the NHS. The NHS—the state—is seen here by 'the public' to be neglectful if not downright cruel to B's best interests.

The costs in terms of pain and suffering to B were felt by her father and stepmother to be bearable in the best interests of her chance of survival. However, they wished to protect her 'from knowledge about her risk of dying' and so B herself was never given the opportunity to give fully informed consent, let alone to refuse treatment. Her rights to be informed and consulted were not upheld. We do not know what B's best interests truly are; only what her parents insisted they must be and what her doctors judged them to be—and the doctors differed. So did the courts, in that the Court of Appeal overturned within 7 hours the judgement of the High Court which had ruled that the district health authority must fund the treatment requested by B's father.[48]

A further, rather different example is given by the national campaign, carried out at the end of last year, to immunise all secondary school children against measles and rubella. This included a laudable drive to obtain written consent from the parent of every child offered immunisation.[49] However, the way in which children themselves were able to consent to the procedure varied throughout the country. In at least one authority, each child was asked whether they had any objections to being immunised and those who refused, even when their parents had consented, were not given the vaccine. This applied to only a handful of children. In some places, children were not offered vaccine if their parents had not given consent. Some schools, chiefly Christian Interdenominational schools, did not want any pupil to be given rubella vaccine because the vaccine is derived from fetal tissue; in these schools, measles vaccine alone was given. The immunisation effort required a great deal of extra time from staff in the community health services for which no extra resources were provided by the Department of Health, although the basic materials were supplied. Local attempts to educate parents about the advantages of vaccination also varied and this aspect in particular received a great deal of criticism from bodies such as the Association of Parents of Vaccine Damaged Children who accused the government of promoting the vaccination by creating fear about the disease.[50] Groups such as these could be accused of using scare tactics themselves. But this illustrates the conflict between some adults' and parents' views and children's rights to be protected from potentially damaging diseases, and the government's responsibility not to withhold immunisation without serious consideration of the effects on the individual child and on the community.

Despite strong pressure from some quarters in the UK, we have so far avoided making pre-school immunisation compulsory to the extent of requiring evidence as a condition for school entry as is required by law in the USA. Many think that this is a failure of the state to provide for all children their entitlement in the face of differing parental views.[51] But in the USA this policy has led to some children not entering school at all and thus missing out on their entitlement to a certain standard and level of education and to the school experience.

The capability of vocal, energetic parents to win resources and influence policy may be laudable in the individual case but risks, as ever, those who are most vulnerable losing out. Some argue that ill health is due primarily to a failure of entitlements such as immunisation rather than to inadequate overall provision.[52] Strengthening entitlements can be done through the law. True implementation of a right means assuring that every individual who is entitled to it gets his or her full share of it. Interests in promoting health can be pursued in many different ways, but to use the language of rights about these interests means that one is going to use the law. But 'ethics cannot be reduced to law'.[41] The law may or may not have upheld B's best interests and using the law is unlikely to ensure children's best interests in matters such as immunisation programmes.

We have seen that very diverse interpretations may be given to the principle of best interests by different individuals and groups, in different settings. A hierarchy of responsibility for a child's best interests has been described:[52]

- Child
- Family centred
- Community
- Local government
- State government
- National government
- International non-governmental organisations
- International governmental organisations

Ideally each agency supports those that are closer to the child but does not substitute for these agencies.

The principle of 'best interests' is complex and is inextricably linked to the cultural context in which is it invoked. At each level in the hierarchy shown above, there may be tensions between the views about children's best interests and the legal constraints; these tensions exist also between levels. Because of the role of government agencies in health care, in deciding on priorities and determining the context in which clinicians treat patients, civil and political rights cannot be divorced from economic, social and cultural rights. The United Nations has always sought to resolve this link which can seem to be overbalanced in one direction or the other, by insisting upon the equal importance of the two sets of rights.

The UN Convention on the Rights of the Child

The UN Convention on the Rights of the Child is a much broader instrument than the Children Act. Ratification does not automatically mean that the Convention becomes law in the UK. The situation is different in the USA where ratification of international treaties automatically brings them into federal law, and although I understand it is about to sign, the USA has not yet ratified the UN Convention.

The UN Convention in itself establishes only what have been called 'soft' rights.[52] They can be transformed into 'hard' rights if national and local governments create suitably strong national and local laws along with effective agencies to implement the rights. 'Hard' rights have a history of case law through which the meaning of the right is tested and refined.

The Convention covers three broad themes: participation, based on the concept of the child as an active and contributing participant in society and not merely as a passive recipient of good or bad treatment; provision, which covers the child's rights to survive and develop by means of an environment and resources such as food, clean water and shelter that allow this, and services such as education and health care; and protection, which deals with all forms of abuse, discrimination and mistreatment, and exploitation of children at work. The Convention is clear that the best place for a child is with its parents, and that the state has a duty to support and assist parents in this responsibility where necessary.[53]

These principles are laid out in three Articles which are of fundamental importance in the implementation of all the others: Article 2, whereby the state must 'respect and ensure' the rights in the Convention for all children without discrimination of any kind on grounds such as disability, race, colour, sex, religion, language, national, ethnic or social origin, birth or other status; Article 3, which states that 'in all actions concerning children, whether undertaken by public or private social welfare institutions, courts of law, administrative authorities or legislative bodies, the best interests of the child shall be a primary consideration'; and Article

12, whereby 'States Parties shall assure to the child who is capable of forming his or her own views the right to express those views freely in all matters affecting the child, the views of the child being given due weight in accordance with the age and maturity of the child'. Article 5 underlines the responsibilities of state and parents to ensure that children are provided with guidance appropriate to their evolving capabilities.

Articles also set out the dimensions of other rights for children. With regard to health and health care, these are principally the child's inherent right to life and the state's duty to ensure to the maximum extent possible the survival and development of the child (Article 6) and Article 24 (Table 1) whereby the child has

Table 1. Article 24 of the UN Convention on the Rights of the Child

1. States Parties recognise the right of the child to the enjoyment of the highest attainable standard of health and to facilities for the treatment of illness and rehabilitation of health. States parties shall strive to ensure that no child is deprived of his or her right of access to such health care services.
2. States Parties shall pursue full implementation of this right and, in particular, shall take appropriate measures:
    (a) to diminish infant and child mortality,
    (b) to ensure the provision of necessary medical assistance and health care of all children with emphasis on the development of primary health care,
    (c) to combat disease and malnutrition including within the framework of primary health care, through inter alia the application of readily available technology and through the provision of adequate nutritious foods and clean drinking water, taking into consideration the dangers and risks of environmental pollution,
    (d) to ensure appropriate pre- and post-natal health care for mothers,
    (e) to ensure that all segments of society, in particular parents and children, are informed, have access to education and are supported in the use of basic knowledge of child health and nutrition, the advantages of breast-feeding, hygiene and environmental sanitation and the prevention of accidents,
    (f) to develop preventive health care, guidance for parents, and family planning education and services.
3. States Parties shall take all effective and appropriate measures with a view to abolishing traditional practices prejudicial to the health of children.
4. States Parties undertake to promote and encourage international co-operation with a view to achieving progressively the full realisation of the right recognised in this article. In this regard, particular account shall be taken of the needs of developing countries.

the right to the enjoyment of the highest attainable standard of health and to facilities for the treatment of illness and for rehabilitation.

In the three years following ratification of the Convention by the UK, a great deal of work was undertaken, much of it by the non-state-funded Children's Rights Development Unit, to find out how current policy and practice fits in with the principles of the Convention.[54] The UK government was required to report on this to the UN Committee on the Rights of the Child at the end of this period.

The UN Committee has now commented upon the UK government's report, noting positively the adoption by 'the State party of a Children's Act applicable to England and Wales . . .'[55] Further positive comments are given in four paragraphs which cover less than one side of an A4 sheet, while the principal subjects of concern cover nearly six sides. The UN Committee expresses particular concerns about the absence of any independent mechanism for the purpose of monitoring developments in relation to the rights of the child; and again, in particular, that the principle of the best interests of the child appears not to be reflected in legislation in such areas as health, education and social security which have a bearing on the respect for the rights of the child.

Covering a whole range of concerns, the UN Committee has identified that in Britain negative or at least not positive attitudes to children are widespread and that their best interests are pursued or perhaps merely safeguarded in ways that are neither comprehensive nor coherent, indeed often conflicting.

In the government's strategy for health in England published in 1992, the importance of the health of infants and children for making progress towards the national targets was highlighted thus: 'Success in meeting the targets will improve the health of children for example in reducing low birth weight associated with expectant mothers smoking during pregnancy, and success with children—for example in establishing healthy lifestyles at a young age—is crucial to the long term success of the strategy.'[56] This strategy has a crucial influence on the priorities for NHS attention and on the markers for achievement in the health service but the health of children is included almost exclusively in relation to its effect on the future health of adults.

As just one comparative example, in France, family policy and legislation have long been centred on the child's best interests.[57] Maternity and welfare benefits are tied to the child's attendance for health preventive and surveillance services. France claims to be the country of human rights 'par excellence', but originally it was the best interests of childhood rather than of the child as such that were served by the legislative. What was lacking in the French system was the right to be heard. However, legislation in recognition of this has now been put high on the national and political agenda. France's report to the UN Committee describes how on every school board there are two children who are trained to ensure that children's rights to express opinions about the running of the school are fully enacted.

The UN Convention on the Rights of the Child reflects sensitivity to the impact of contextual factors and cultural considerations on the norms it purports to set. As shown in the hierarchy of responsibility, the international community should help national governments in their work with children. This mirrors the requirements of comprehensive needs assessment in health care commissioning.[28] The tensions may seem so acute in the UK because the variation in the local situation is often so great and local administrative boundaries do not follow lines of population variation or necessarily of political influence.

A large number of people and interests have the power to decide what is in children's best interests. How can acting towards children with the objective of furthering their best interests (which the UN Convention says must be 'a primary consideration' in all actions concerning children) be reconciled with treating children as possessors of rights (which the UN Convention clearly thinks they are). These two bases for action require reconciliation if the argument is accepted that a right that another should have complete power to determine what is in A's interests and to direct A accordingly leaves A without any rights at all. They can be reconciled by allowing scope for the child to determine what those interests are; this has been called 'dynamic self-determinism'.[58] It is more than merely an application of Article 12 of the Convention affording the child the right to express his or her views, and allows for changes in the child's views—or in children's views—over time. It must be an incremental and iterative process.

It has come to be realised that the dichotomy between protecting children and protecting their rights is false. Children who are not protected, whose welfare is not advanced, will not be able to exercise self-determination. On the other hand, a failure to recognise the personalities of children is likely to result in undermining their protection and reducing them to objects of intervention.

Learning from young people

Finally, I want to give a few examples of what we can learn from what children and young people tell us. A 14 year old girl published an account in the *British Medical Journal* of the time she underwent chemotherapy two years previously.[59] She wrote of her feelings of isolation and terror each time she went for treatment:

> When that vile yellow toxin was linked to my arm I could make myself sick by just watching it ooze down the tube and into my body . . . On that table is the only time I can truly say that if I could have stood up I would have killed myself. The feeling of utter hopelessness, frustration, and boredom led to desperation I never, ever want to experience again.

She also described how simple measures, such as a video to help distract her during the treatment process and attention paid to the special needs of older children in the way the department was run, would have helped enormously.

Second, patients with brittle diabetes place an enormous burden upon the resources of the health service and cause physical, psychological and often financial strain to themselves and their families.[60] It is widely considered by workers in the field that maladaptive behaviour is the commonest cause of brittle diabetes, often remaining undetected after exhaustive investigation has excluded other potential causes such as inappropriate treatment of insulin-dependent diabetes or undiagnosed intercurrent illness. The key element is extreme fluctuations in metabolic control sufficient to cause disruption to the lifestyle or to endanger the life of a patient. Young people with this condition indulge in potentially dangerous behaviour, partly because they are ignorant as to its consequences but more often because it 'pays' in the sense of fulfilling other needs whether for love, shelter, approval or escape from an otherwise insoluble conflict.

Deaf children, in growing up, may or may not make the choice to learn to speak so as to fit into 'normal' society—the hearing world—as their parents and professional carers almost inevitably would want. But within this hearing society, a deaf person is likely to remain disabled. The choice may be made to concentrate on learning to sign and to grow up as a fully competent member of the world of the deaf—in which those who cannot sign are disabled.[61]

A final example comes from the work of the Council for Disabled Children.[62] Through a voluntary organisation, young people with disabilities were offered a unique opportunity to talk through with a peer group how they actually perceived themselves. These young people found it extraordinarily difficult to acknowledge their own disabilities. They all felt they had been given very little factual information about their special health care or disability problems. When asked if they would make a presentation to their parents, who were members of local voluntary organisations for carers, none of them felt confident to say what it felt like growing up with a disability. However, they prepared a composite figure called Miss Can—with her down side Miss Can't—to express what they felt, and these figures illustrate something of what we can learn about the needs of these young people and the requirements for disability services.

Miss Can was invented by a young women's group and was tall, slim and clever—the sort of person they thought they wanted to be. She could be any teenager; she goes jogging and wears fashionable clothes; she has a boyfriend and is buying a house; she works as a mechanic fixing cars; she writes music and sings in a band; she can ride a bike, drive a car, run fast, write neatly, buy a video, play the piano, swim and dive, and rob a bank. This last possibility was in reaction to the heavy onus we place on people who have disabilities, and their carers, on being deserving. When services are scarce and are being rationed, people feel that they have to be good enough to get the services.

Miss Can't is how the young people presented themselves in what they felt was the real world: a young lady who cannot walk easily and needs crutches, who gets puffed out and cannot touch her toes; she is fat and podgy and eats too many sweets; she lives with her parents and her mum looks after her; she stays at home all the time unless she gets her brother to take her out; she is behind at school because the teacher takes no notice of her because she has learning difficulties; she has to go to school in a special bus, a disabled bus; she is slow at writing, stupid at maths, cannot use money, cannot find her way around, and has a miserable life. These are extremes, but many young adolescent girls see themselves in a very negative way. And there are some powerful messages about how the parents perceived their young adult children. These young people were not allowed to go out because it was not thought to be safe; brothers and sisters had to accompany them and had worked out a nice bribery system to get paid for doing it. These young people really perceived themselves as disabled, although they were not significantly so in many people's eyes.

We may not find it easy to understand, let alone to give proper attention to, these kinds of expression of what is important to children and young people. But we cannot afford not to do so. It is a field that we have been forced to enter notably in child sexual abuse following the work of Alice Miller, describing the devastating effects on children, persisting as they grow up, of not being able to disclose what they have experienced.[63]

Work with teenagers shows not only widespread disenchantment with the world in which they are growing up but also concern and a sense of responsibility for their own actions and for society. They show particular concern for the environment, albeit expressed in uncompromising language as at a conference on teenage health held in Birmingham in April 1992, where a local teenager spoke thus about what it was like to be a teenager today.[64]

> The kids where I live don't give a shit about their parents or anybody or anything. Your generation messed up the country. Look at the ozone layer and that. You've messed up the earth and we're going to have to pay for it soon. Stop trying to improve other people and improve yourselves.

The director of Demos, the independent think-tank, has recently commented that ours is an age where inherited duties and commandments have lost their pull.[65] Today, for better or worse, everyone is brought up to question and to contest, and to think about ethics in much more personal terms. This may be why a more personal language of responsibility, rooted not in duty but in individual choices and values each of us learns and experiences through school and life, fits much better with the times.

Children do not only tell us difficult things. We must not forget how much we have learned, in addition to disease processes and to impairments arising in childhood, about the magic in children, about their desire and energy for exploration, about their inventiveness and imagination. These are not only of incomparable value—if they can be expressed—to the individual, but to the capacity of the human race to adapt to a changing world, hopefully to enjoy greater richness in the experience of living. Above all, I believe that the essence of childhood exists in these qualities and that the human race depends on the continuing existence of such a childhood if it is to survive.

References

1. Bennett A. *The Madness of George III*. London: Faber, 1995 (first published 1992).
2. Macalpine I, Hunter R. *George III and the 'Mad Business'*. London: Allen Lane, 1969.
3. Freeman MDA. Taking children's rights seriously. *Children and Society* 1987–88; **4**: 299–319.

4. Brown GH (ed). *Lives of the Fellows of the Royal College of Physicians of London 1826–1925.* London: Royal College of Physicians, 1995.
5. Court D, Alberman E. Worlds apart. In: Forfar J (ed). *Child Health in a Changing Society.* London: British Paediatric Association, 1988, pp 1–30.
6. Loudon I. *Death in Childbirth. An International Study of Maternal Care and Maternal Mortality 1800–1950.* Oxford: Clarendon Press, 1992.
7. Kosky J. *Mutual Friends: Charles Dickens and Great Ormond Street Children's Hospital.* London: Weidenfeld and Nicholson, 1989.
8. Woodroffe, Glickman M, Barker M, Power C. *Children, Teenagers and Health. The Key Data.* Buckingham and Philadelphia: Open University Press, 1993.
9. Ariès P. *Centuries of Childhood.* Penguin, 1973.
10. Riché P, Alexandre-Bidon D. *L'enfance au Moyen Age.* Seuil: Bibliothèque nationale de France, 1994.
11. Department of Health and Social Security, Department of Education and Science and Welsh Office. *Fit for the Future: Report of the Committee on Child Health Services* (Chair: Professor Donald Court). London: HMSO, 1976.
12. Stone L. *The Family, Sex and Marriage in England 1500–1800.* London: Weidenfeld and Nicholson, 1977.
13. Qvortrup J (ed). *Childhood as a Social Phenomenon: Lessons from an International Project.* Report of a Conference in Billund, Denmark, in September 1992. European Centre for Social Welfare Policy and Research and the Sydjysk Universitetscenter, Bergasse 17, 1090 Vienna, Austria, 1993.
14. Halsey AH. Changes in the family. *Children and Society* 1993; **7**(2): 125–36.
15. Department of Health. *The NHS Patient's Charter.* London: HMSO, April 1992.
16. *The Citizen's Charter.* London: HMSO, July 1991.
17. Department of Health. *An Introduction to the Children Act 1989.* London: HMSO, 1989.
18. Rutter M, Smith D (eds). *Psychological Disorders in Young People: Time Trends and their Causes.* Chichester: Wiley, 1994.
19. Phillimore P, Beattie A, Townsend P. Widening inequality of health in northern England, 1981–91. *British Medical Journal* 1994; **308**: 1125–8.
20. Wadsworth M, Kuh D. Are gains in child health being undermined? *Developmental Medicine and Child Neurology* 1993; **35**: 742–5.
21. *Inquiry into Income and Wealth.* A report sponsored by the Joseph Rowntree Foundation, 1995.
22. Graham P. Social class, social disadvantage and child health. *Children and Society* 1988; **2**(1): 9–19.
23. Secretaries of State for Health and for Wales. *Children Act Report 1992.* London: HMSO, 1993.
24. Kurtz Z, Thornes R, Wolkind S. *Services for the Mental Health of Children and Young People in England: a National Review.* South Thames Regional Health Authority, 1994.
25. Audit Commission. *Getting in on the Act. Provision for Pupils with Special Needs: the National Picture.* London: HMSO, 1992.
26. Association of Metropolitan Authorities (AMA). *Special Child: Special Needs. Services for Children with Disabilities.* London: AMA, 1994.

27. Townsend D. For the smelly, dirty and dying. Definition of neglect could help prevent child death. *Guardian* 15 March 1995, Society Section p 2.
28. National Health Service Management Executive. *Assessing Health Care Needs*. A DHA project discussion paper, 1991.
29. Mayall B. Childcare and childhood. *Children and Society* 1990; **4**(4): 374–85.
30. Pugh G, De'Ath E, Smith C. *Confident Parents, Confident Children. Policy and Practice in Parent Education and Support*. London: National Children's Bureau, 1994.
31. Winnicott DW. *The Child, the Family, and the Outside World*. Penguin, 1994.
32. Wolkind SN. The 1989 Children Act. A cynical view from an ivory tower. *ACPP Review and Newsletter* 1993; **15**(1): 40–1.
33. Meslin EM, Lemieux-Charles L, Wortley JT. *Teaching Clinician-Managers How to Address Ethical Issues in Resource Allocation Decisions. Resource Package*. Technical Report No. 16. May, 1994. Hospital Management Research Unit, Department of Health Administration, Faculty of Medicine, University of Toronto, Canada.
34. Goldstein J, Freud A, Solnit AJ, Goldstein S. *In the Best Interests of the Child*. New York: The Free Press, 1986.
35. Mnookin R. *In the Interest of Children: Advocacy, Law Reform and Public Policy*. New York: WH Freeman, 1985.
36. Department of Health. *Welfare of Children and Young People in Hospital*. London: HMSO, 1991.
37. Rogers MC. Pain relief in infants and children. *New England Journal of Medicine* 1992; **326**: 55–6.
38. Alderson P, Goodwin M. Contradictions within concepts of children's competence. *International Journal of Children's Rights* 1993; **1**(3–4): 303–13.
39. Mitchels B, Prince A. *The Children Act and Medical Practice*. Bristol: Jordan Family Law, 1992.
40. Children under 14 not capable of crime. Law report. *Independent* 21 March 1995.
41. Mahowald MB. *Women and Children in Health Care: An Unequal Majority*. New York: Oxford University Press, 1993.
42. Moshman D. Book reviews of:
   Flavell JH, Miller PH, Miller SA. *Cognitive Development*, 3rd edn. Englewood Cliffs, NJ, USA: Prentice-Hall, 1993.
   Meadows S. *The Child as Thinker: the Development and Acquisition of Cognition in Childhood*. London and New York: Routledge, 1993.
   Rosser R. *Cognitive Development: Psychological and Biological Perspectives*. Boston: Allyn and Bacon, 1994.
   In: *International Journal of Children's Rights* 1994; **2**: 235–337.
43. Withholding of treatment for cancer upheld. Law report. *Independent* 14 March 1995.
44. Hall C. Child B to have newly developed treatment. *Independent* 5 April 1995.
45. Hopkins A (ed). *Measures of the Quality of Life and the Uses to which Such Measures may be Put*. London: Royal College of Physicians, 1992.

46. Clinical Standards Advisory Group. *Childhood Leukaemia. Access to and Availability of Specialist Services.* Report of a working group (chair: Dr John Lilleyman). London: HMSO, 1993.

47. *The NAWCH Charter for Children in Hospital.* London: Action for Sick Children (formerly NAWCH), 1994. Now republished as *Ten Targets for the 1990s,* May 1992.

48. Cancer girl loses fight for treatment. *Independent* 11 March 1995.

49. Department of Health. *National Measles and Rubella Immunisation Campaign.* Heywood (Lancashire): Department of Health, 1994 (Professional Letter: PL/CMO(94)10).

50. Association of Parents of Vaccine Damaged Children. *The Criteria for Effective and Responsible Promotion of Vaccination.* Obtainable from the Hon. Sec, 2 Church Street, Shipston on Stour CV36 4AP.

51. Bedford H. Should immunisation be a requirement for school entry? *Maternal and Child Health* 1991; **16**(1): 2–5.

52. Kent G. Children's rights to adequate nutrition. *International Journal of Children's Rights* 1993; **1**: 133–54.

53. Lindsay MJ. *An Introduction to Children's Rights.* Highlight No. 1133. London: National Children's Bureau, 1992.

54. Lansdown G, Newell P (eds). *UK Agenda for Children.* London: Children's Rights Development Unit, April 1994.

55. United Nations Committee on the Rights of the Child. Consideration of Reports submitted by States Parties under Article 14 of the Convention at the eighth session. January 1995.

56. Secretary of State for Health. *The Health of the Nation.* London: HMSO, 1992.

57. Rubellin-Devichi J. The best interests principle in French law and practice. In: Alston P (ed). *The Best Interests of the Child. Reconciling Culture and Human Rights.* UNICEF, Oxford: Clarendon Press, 1994: 259–80.

58. Eckelaar J. The interests of the child and the child's wishes: The role of dynamic self-determination. In: Alston P (ed). *The Best Interests of the Child. Reconciling Culture and Human Rights.* UNICEF, Oxford: Clarendon Press, 1994: 42–66.

59. Anonymous. Easing a childhood nightmare: personal view. *British Medical Journal* 1990; **301**: 244.

60. Tattersall RB, Walford S. Brittle diabetes in response to life stress. Cheating and Manipulation. In: Pickup JC (ed) *Brittle Diabetes.* Oxford: Blackwell Scientific Publications, 1985: 76–102.

61. Cayton H. *Children, Ears and Aristotle.* Speech given at a conference in Athens in November 1987 on the Education of Deaf Children. In the published proceedings obtainable from the National Deaf Children's Society, pp 16–21.

62. Russell P. The role of voluntary organisations. In: Kurtz Z, Hopkins A (eds). *Services for Young People with Chronic Disorders in their Transition from Childhood to Adult Life.* Royal College of Physicians (in press).

63. Miller A. *Though Shalt Not Be Aware.* UK: Pluto Press, 1990.

64. Smith R. Leader. *British Medical Journal* 1992; **304**: 1001.

65. Mulgan G. Beyond the lure of off-the-shelf ethics. Essay. *The Independent,* 30 January 1995, p 13.